CARVING HAWK

✳

ALSO BY MAURICE KENNY

In the Time of the Present (2000)
Tortured Skins & Other Fictions (2000)
Common Days: A Place Record (1998)
Backward to Forward (Essays, 1997)
On Second Thought (1995)
Last Mornings In Brooklyn (1991)
Tekonwatonti: Molly Brant (1992)
Rain and Other Fictions (Stories, 1990)
The Short and the Long of It (1990)
Greyhounding This America (1988)
Humors and/or Not So Humorous (1988)
Between Two Rivers (1987)
Is Summer This Bear (1985)
The Mama Poems (1984)
Blackrobe: Isaac Jogues (1982)
The Smell of Slaughter (1982)
Boston Tea Party (1982)
Kneading the Blood (1981)
Only As Far As Brooklyn (1979)
Dancing Back Strong the Nation (1979)
North: Poems of Home (1977)
I Am The Sun (1976)
With Love to Lesbia (1960)
Dead Letters Sent (1958)
The Hopeless Kill (1958)

EDITED BY MAURICE KENNY
Stories for a Winter's Night (2000)
Wounds Beneath the Flesh (1987)

CARVING HAWK

New & Selected Poems
1953–2000

Maurice Kenny

WHITE PINE PRESS ❖ BUFFALO, NEW YORK

Grateful acknowledgment is made to the presses which first published the volumes included in this book, including: Michigan State University Press, University of Oklahoma Press, University of Arkansas Press, White Pine Press, North Country Community College Press, Blue Cloud Quarterly Press, Soup Press, Strawberry Press, Good Gay Poets, dodeca, Troubador Press, and Akwesasne Notes.

With gratitude to Karoniaktatie, Will Roscoe, Joe and Carol Bruchac, Geary Hobson, Philip Foss, Duane Niatum, Alan Velie, Jan Bender, Jan Garden Castro, Michael Castro, Murray Heller, Madge Heller, Frank Parman, Judy Grahn, Larry Jackson, Robin Kay Willoughby, Chris Shaw, Clifford Trafzer, Mark Nowak, Diane Glancy, Dan Bodah, Rochelle Ratner, Ken Warren, Thomas King, Craig Lesley, Brian Swann and Arnold Krupat, Sarah Iselin, A. Lavonne Ruoff, Jose Berrario, Dan (Rokwaho) Thompson, Robert K. Martin, Barry Silesky, Ric Henry, Charlie Shively, Charles Williams, Ed Foster, Annette Tanner, Chris Angus, Laure-Anne Bosselaar, Gerald Vizenor, James Ruppert, Steve Levandowski, Bro. Benet Tvedten, Bertha Rodgers, and Beatrice Machet—and my faithful typist, C.C. Martin.

Publication of this book was made possible, in part, by grants from the National Endowment for the Arts and with public money from the New York State Council on the Arts, a State Agency.

Cover drawing: Danielle Cole

Printed and bound in the United States of America.

Published by
White Pine Press, P.O. Box 236, Buffalo, NY 14201
www.whitepine.org

First Edition

ISBN 1-893996-50-6

Library of Congress Control Number: 2002106768

✳ CONTENTS

Preface / 15

✳ THE HOPELESS KILL (1956), DEAD LETTERS SENT (1958), and WITH LOVE TO LESBIA (1960)

Truth: the Search / 23
Resignation / 25
Ritual / 26
A Walk in the City / 27
I Will Learn to Bear the Sting of Fire / 28
The Hopeless Kill / 29
Dead Letters Sent / 30
The Hawk / 34
To Lesbia from Catullus, 1958 / 35
Catullus to Lesbia, 1958 / 35

✳ I AM THE SUN (1976)

I Am The Sun / 39
I See With My Own Eyes / 43

✳ NORTH: POEMS OF HOME (1977)

First Rule / 49
Gowane / 50
Cold Creek / 52
Home / 53
Mulleins Are My Arms / 55
Land / 56

✳ DANCING BACK STRONG THE NATION (1979)

    Listen, the old woman came here / 61
    I Went North / 62
    Drums / 63
    The Women / 64
    Dance / 65
    Moccasin / 66
    Going Home / 68
    The Steelworker / 69
    Legacy / 70
    Yaikini / 72
    In My Sixth August / 74
    Wild Strawberry / 75
    Faye / 77
    In the Flow / 78

✳ ONLY AS FAR AS BROOKLYN (1981)

    Boys / 81
    I Shall Not Write of Love / 82
    Winkte / 83
    Papago I / 85
    Papago II / 86
    After Reading The Greek Poet / 87
    Comanche of the Yamaha / 88
    Kodachrome Double Exposure / 89

✳ KNEADING THE BLOOD (1981)

    Strawberrying / 93
    The Parts We Keep / 94

✳ BOSTON TEA PARTY (1982)

> Boston Tea Party / 99

✳ THE SMELL OF SLAUGHTER (1982)

> Sacrifice / 107
> Boyhood Country Creek / 108
> They Tell Me I Am Lost / 109
> In Country Light / 112
> Oh, Wendy, Arthur / 113
> Horses / 114

✳ BLACKROBE (1982)

> Peacemaker / 117
> Aiionwatha / 118
> Rouen, France / 119
> At Sea / 120
> Les Hures / 121
> First Meeting With Kiotsaeton / 122
> Kiotsaeton / 124
> Cardinal Richelieu / 125
> Approaching the Mohawk Village / 126
> Bear (One) / 127
> Among the Mohawks / 128
> The People of the Flint / 129
> Wolf Aunt (One) / 130
> Wolf Aunt (Two) / 131
> His Visions / 134
> Bear (Two)/ 136
> October 18, 1646 / 139
> The French Informal Report / 140
> Turtle / 141
> Tekawitha / 143
> Rokwaho / 144

✳ THE MAMA POEMS (1984)

    1911 / 147
    Coming to an Understanding / 149
    Sometimes, Injustice / 150
    Mama Failed to Kill the Rat / 151
    Inheritance / 152
    Wake / 153
    Picking Blackberries / 154
    Joshua Clark / 156
    Black River, Summer 1981 / 160
    Telephone Call / 162
    Mama / 164
    December / 167
    May 15, 1982 / 168
    Reverberation / 170
    1982 / 171

✳ IS SUMMER THIS BEAR (1985)

    Osheranoha / 175
    12 Moons / 176
    Wolf / 177
    Redtail / 178
    Listening for the Elders / 180
    Graveyards / 182
    Kaherawak's Birthday / 184

✳ GREYHOUNDING THIS AMERICA (1988)

    A Partial Explanation / 189
    For Cherokee Marie / 190
    Sand Creek, Colorado / 191
    The Yellowstone / 193
    Monet / 197
    When in Reality / 198
    Canyon de Chelly, Return, 1978 / 199
    November Sierras, 1976 / 201
    Wanda on the Seashore / 202
    Reading Poems in Public / 203

✳ HUMORS AND/OR NOT SO HUMOROUS (1988)

    On Second Thought / 207
    Heard Poem / 208
    The Comet / 209
    Young Male / 210
    Sofky: Seminole Soup / 212
    Friendship Days at Akwesasne / 213
    Ojibwa / 214
    Oroville High, California / 215
    Inuit / 216
    Reno Hill...Little Bighorn / 217
    Listening to Leslie Silko Telling Stories / 218

✳ THE SHORT AND THE LONG OF IT (1990)

    In The Vines / 221
    Postcard / 223
    Walking Woods With Dogs / 229
    Mysteries / 232
    Dugout / 235

✳ Last Mornings in Brooklyn (1991)

    Saturday Morning Between 7 A.M. and 12 Noon / 251
        7 A.M....
        The yellow Honda
        It's a hot day...
        His t-shirt...
        A youth...
        Apollo and David...
        Helene pushes Evan's carriage...
        His hawk feather
        I know his name is Browning,...
        Norman Mailer...
        He stands, he leans,...

✳ Tekonwatonti: Molly Brant (1992)

    I, Tekonwatonti / 257
    Molly Brant to Willie / 259
    Sir William's Reply to Molly / 260
    Molly: Report Back to the Village / 261
    General Jeffrey Amherst / 262
    Sir William Johnson: On His Death Bed / 263
    Molly: At His Death / 264
    Molly / 265
    Call Me...Woman / 267

✳ On Second Thought (1995)

    For Brett / 271
    Recuerdo / 272
    Sunflower / 273
    On the Jetty / 274

✳ COMMON DAYS: A PLACE RECORD (1998)

    Spring / 277
    Michael / 277
    Van of Students / 277
    My Lynn (W) / 278
    Wildflower / 279
    Above the Saranac / 280
    Ghosts / 281
    Sula / 282

✳ IN THE TIME OF THE PRESENT (2000)

    New Song / 285
    Photograph / 286
    Roman Nose: Cheyenne Warrior / 289
    O/Rain in the Face / 292
    Mask / 294
    The Hands of Annie-Mae Aquash / 296
    Mood Piece / 299
    Writing a Love Letter I Know You Will Never Receive / 300
    "Why is Scarface Your Favorite Mountain?" / 302
    Sweat / 303
    Pima / 306
    Dancing at Oneida Nation / 307
    An American Night / 308
    Christmas / 309
    The Note / 311
    Tekonwatonti, German Flats / 314
    Essence / 315

✳ UNCOLLECTED POEMS (2001)

Visiting Elaine / 319
Going to the Mountains / 322
Sky Woman / 324
Still Life at Cedar House / 327
Tongue-Tied / 328
Cudweed / 329
Chokeberry / 333
Indominitable Spirit / 334
Stone Throwing / 336
Reflected Eberhart / 338
Gold / 339
You Know Who You Were, Are, Will Be / 343
Words to the Indian Woman of the West Coast / 346
Okanagan / 348
El Paso Del Norte / 349
Allen Ginsberg / 352
Andrew's Dilemma / 355
Feo/Bello / 356
Existential Dread / 358
Detail / 362
Maurice Kenny: A Brief Biography / 364

✳

For Eva and John Fadden, and their father Ray;
Thuy and Nick, Dean and Lori
          and their energies;
Sarah Iselin and Frank Parman;
Quino; Jenna, my surrogate niece;
Elaine and Dennis
          and their creative beauties;
Brother Benet Tvedten
          for the faith and the labors;
Martha, my favorite niece,
          and Steve, her good man;
the very special Neal Burdick
and the extra special Carole Ashkinaze;
Ruth Woodward and Paul Rosado;
Kathleen Leone and Jamie Kincaid;
Eleanor Sweeney, Tim and Diana Fortune;
John Radigan and Alan Steinberg, a great boss;
Jeremy Reidhe, for Lucy's sake;
Rob Wagner and Adam Pallack,
          my buddies, my highwaymen
          and for being such good students;
and for Martha Bates, my editor;
and never to forget—in memory
Diane Decorah and Lorne Simon,
Mary Dickson, Fred Hoch, and Barbara Cameron,
my best high school friend, Joe White,
and Agnes Marie Kenny LaMora
and Mary Kenny Mothersell, my sisters.

✳ PREFACE

Long before I became a permanent resident in the Adirondacks
at Saranac Lake, I often went to visit John and Eva Fadden, then,
as now, living in the tiny mountain community of Onchiota, a
hamlet of some sixty souls, "and one sorehead," as the road sign
tells the wary tourist. The Faddens, true Iroquois-Mohawks origi-
nally from Akwesasne Reserve, live on a large acreage of wooded
land, mainly conifers and richly lush with wild berries and moun-
tain animals such as bear, turtle, coyote, raccoon, rabbit, fisher,
and others. There is also a plethora of birds: bluejays, cardinals,
even a vulture or two, and many red-tailed hawks; an eagle has
been sighted in their woods. Some fifty-odd years ago John's
father, Ray Fadden (known to the Native Community as
Tehanetorens), who'd been a science teacher for many years, com-
menced collecting Indian culture, lore, art, old canoes, photos,
and other memorabilia to be housed in a museum financially sup-
ported solely by his own hand. The museum is called Six Nations
Indian Museum, after the Six Nations which comprise the Iroquois
Confederacy, or Great League, founded by Deganawidah, a Huron
and a cultural hero. The museum has flourished; its collection
covers walls, floors and ceilings. It is richly valuable in culture,
impressive, and the museum entertains and informs, as all good
Native stories must do.

John and Eva Fadden are both fine artists, as is Ray. John is a world-renowned painter. His drawings are world famous. Eva is a sculptor in both wood and soapstone. Her sculpture is in great demand, and herwork is purchased almost before the piece is completed.

I've visited the Faddens many times and there in the woods many insights and images for poems developed from talks and walks, smells, sights, and sounds. One spring I rode Greyhound north from Brooklyn, where I was then living, to Saranac Lake and continued on by automobile to Onchiota. Upon arriving at the Fadden's home, I rushed into the house to greet Eva and sip a cup of her coffee from the pot which is always warm on the stove. I entered the kitchen. It was empty. Eva was elsewhere in the house. Taking a seat at the kitchen table, relaxed from the long bus ride, I allowed my gaze to wander the room. First, a collection of family photos on the walls. Far off in the right corner stood a narrow but high storage cabinet. To my utter surprise, pleasure, and bewilderment, I was struck dumb at the sight of a red-tailed hawk perched on top of that very cabinet.

At first a choke at the throat, and then I heard myself call out to Eva that there was a hawk in her kitchen. I remembered knowingly that Ray Fadden, her father-in-law, often found wounded birds on the forest floor and would gently, cautiously bring them home to heal a broken wing or leg, or to extract a fishhook from a beak. Ray is very well known in the area for tending and feeding the animals, reptiles and birds—the very earth and all Mother Earth holds in her womb on turtle's back. Eva entered the kitchen. She is always calm and gentle, quiet, but her words are potent. She is also a very pretty woman, and mother of three artistic sons. She entered the room, went to fill a coffee cup for me, and turned to smile at my exhilaration concerning the hawk on the cabinet.

"He's only wood. I finished carving this morning."

Come to find out, she had been commissioned by Salli Benedict, then the director of the Akwasasne Museum on the reserve at Hogansburg, to carve the Iroquois clan fetishes for the museum. And thus hawk sat on the cabinet. I was astounded yet thrilled by the marvelous talent of this very enchanting woman. Here the poem "Karonhisake"

carving hawks
in her kitchen
and
wolves
turtles
bears
as she becomes
"Searching Sky"

Searching Sky is Eva's Mohawk name, Karonhisake, in English.

The hawk is a clan of the Seneca Nation and is considered most important in legend as the hawk is messenger to the spirit world above. Having learned of the legend of the hawk, my young friend and volunteer typist, Dan Bodah—a fine poet in his own right—encouraged me to title this collection *Carving Hawk* instead of a tentative title I had earlier decided on: *Visiting Elaine*, Elaine being my darling friend, Elaine LaMattina. Many visits have been made over the years to Elaine's attractive kitchen; many apple pies and coffees, many words exchanged late into many nights. Our rapport never seems to finish; there's always something left to say in the morning over yet more coffee.

I thought *Visiting Elaine* would make a striking and memorable title for this collection. But the more I pondered, the more I began to realize that the title should hint of home in the Adirondacks and of Native culture. Dan and I spent several hours going over the poems included to pick out of the lines a title. Nothing appealed to us but *Carving Hawk*. As spirituality is the center of Iroquois traditional culture, and as said the hawk is a messenger, and as Eva Fadden is such a talented, proficient carver/artist, the decision was made to use the line from the poem "Karonhisake" to celebrate "the spirit," the hawk, Eva herself, and womanhood.

There are numerous people I wish to thank for contributions to *Carving Hawk* or for other sorts of support. First, Rachel Guido deVries, Director of the Community Writers' Project, who generously helped funnel finances into my hand; the New York State Council on the Arts for the residency bestowed in 1992; and Poets and Writers, Inc., which has offered much support over the years; Neal Burdick and Joy Neiven, who have also aided me, and the high school students at the annual International Writers Conference of St. Lawrence University; Sandra Orie, who offered a residency at Green Bay, Wisconsin, and the Menominie Reserve in Wisconsin. And Diane Wager from Little Falls.

A special thanks is due to Dan Bodah, who diligently typed, though at times his back felt near breaking. He's a good scout, fine experimental poet and developing into an astute editor. Without Brett Sanchi I could never have taken the trips/tours across country in search of an audience. Brett not only watered the African violet and collected mail but took Sula and Lucy, my cats, under his wing for care. And Dennis Maloney, my friend and publisher, who has kept faith in my pen these many years and many books later.

Few books come strictly from the imagination or brain without help and some who have pumped the juices were Chad, Todd, Dean, Deborah, Lorraine, Peg, Nina, Suzanne—all former students, now friends; others are certainly John and Eva, Larry and Jennifer, Joe and Vickie, Wendy and Arthur, Wanda and Julian, Frank and Sarah, Rochelle and George, Allan and Sue, Mary and David (for our great writers' summer weeks), Alan Steinberg, Jeannette Armstrong, who brought me to the pleasures of the En'Owkin Center in British Columbia, and my card-playing buddies Florene, Michael and the late but beautiful, handsome and most talented Lorne Simon; and Gail Rogers Rice who is precious to us all. And a thank you to Laura Mahon, Jen Yarrow, and Michelle Mullen is in order.

Writing anything creative is very difficult work. It takes time from mountain hiking and climbing; it deprives friends of your company and you the joy of theirs; time from reading—a constant enchantment; from letter writing to family and friends far away; even from keeping the house spotless—hence eternal gratitude to all the above who have given—and given up—so much so that a new poem, a story or an essay may enter the world.

—Maurice Kenny
In the Adirondacks

THE HOPELESS KILL, DEAD LETTERS SENT AND WITH LOVE TO LESBIA

TRUTH: THE SEARCH

I've hunted you in every corner, close and far,
And saw you go into the dark and hide behind the moon,
The stars and even once behind the rising sun.
I sought you in the violet, the oak, the vulture's prey,
About the stone of Gettysburg, and in the precious gold
Of old Byzantium. I've marched to the depths of angry seas,
And picked my way along the soaring clifty mountain paths.
There was a time I thought I had you by the throat...that day
I dusted off the shelf and re-arranged my books, but when
I lurched you ran away like some small elf or water nymph,
Haughty and spoiled on play. There wasn't anything or anyplace
I overlooked! I cut a sparrow's breast and plucked her heart;
I ate a berry, red and ripe, so sweet I yearned to sit
And eat and eat all day. I looked in brooding clouds,
The snows, the rains, and things that come and go and have
No names. I thought you in the wind, the triumphant sea,
Asleep within a temple's musty hall; but you
Ran faster than my foot, my thought. I ripped the earth
In spurts of rage; I halved the sea, the air and fire;
I smashed an atom once, and sanded down a crucifix to find
You there.
            But there was nothing left to do but yield, give up
The silly chase, despair, and wish upon the moon. You were
A dream within a dream that comes tomorrow eve. You were
Like gods of mythic Rome...a figment of my inner-brain.

I came to be the winder of the clocks, and age became my key.
I settled for a rocker on a porch, a garden full of peonies,
And rain to wash the April mud away.

And soon they had me on the bed...puffed out and fat
With drugs (wanting to cheat me of the drama of the scene)
But not so drugged that when the altar boy passed by

I could not look upon his candlestick and see
Your fleeting face, then bright and young and plump
Within that one and simple flash of light that spurted from
The candle's flame onto the holder's gloss. I saw,
And held you then...a moment just before the end...I saw myself.

RESIGNATION

The voiceless pines
Have no anger, cannot shout
At the wind as it rages
Through needles and limbs.

The quiet hum of the plundered pine,
Raped as though a closed-eyed child,
Only lifts or lowers its tone
But does not scream
Its brutal violation.

Open your arms, old mountain pine,
Accept
The cry and the lash and the hate
Of the crazed wind
Which loves you.

Ritual

Wild rose burning, self sacrificed,
This ritual continues: the invocation of
       taut
Stem, leaf, petal to sun and rain
And right wind to carry forward
To countless senses this last
Sacrifice of self, total being...
This strength, this scent, this bloom.

The obsidian night will gash, tear out
The last stronghold of all its freshness.
Once more, the gods appeased,
Bloody bloom will stain this golden altar
Made of mountain stone.

A Walk in the City

Rain,
And the red
Neon
Bobbing
On the rain
Drops,
Splashing down
The ugly face
Of night.

12 o'clock
And 42nd St.
Is empty as a rat
Hole
When there is cheese
On a plate,
Desolate
Except
For a yellow blur
A drenched madonna
Thought to be
A cab.

Hell
Does not scream
Any
Louder
Than this circle long
Mirror
Of sick
Nobodies
Caught
Between showers
On the street
Of dimes
Where even the tinsel
Does not tinkle
When the tiny gongs
Of rain
Strike.

I Will Learn To Bear The Sting Of Fire

I will learn to bear the sting of fire
As I have learned to bear the scent of flowers;
A blaze of fire
Is nothing
Compared to love.

I will learn to bear the lonely wind of October
As I have learned to bear the last morning star;
The wind in the fields
Away down the road beyond,
This wind is nothing
Compared to love.

But love I will
Not ever learn to bear
Whether
It be kind
Or rough like wind...
Spreading
And shaking the lonely hills...
Whether it leap like fire
In desire
Or sing
Like an alien whippoorwill.

THE HOPELESS KILL

I went to the forest with my ax
To break the neck of a copperhead.
I found the sleek and languid thing
Entangled round a hemlock tree.
His eyes, mere firing flames,
Were peering at a hummingbird
A foot away. I crept across
The autumn haze, could smell the pine
And ferns, and saw a puccoon's white
Shadow illuminate a chip
Of brittle shale.
            I lunged. The ax
Came plunging down. It struck him just
Below the brownish head. He coiled
About the hemlock's trunk; unwound,
And spat his green and evil cud...

I laughed. The thing I sought to kill
Was there on embryonic earth,
Was drowning in a pool of blood.
The copperhead was dead. But then
It was too soon to know its mate,
Behind the camouflage of ferns,
Was hatching eggs of many sons.
Nor did I stop to realize
That I must soon return to stalk
The April woods, must live to kill,
To drop the bloody ax again.

DEAD LETTERS SENT
(By the Ontario shores)
I.

Now the clover greens the long meadow
Running the brook to the sweep of the rising hills;
The corn and wheat, which I have sown
These past few weeks, have shown their first green tongues
Of life; the pear orchard and the leafless patch of vines
Have been pruned and sprayed and there has been
Some time to plant a few hollyhocks
At the gate and some yellow columbine
At the edge of the road. Now there are long
Moments to think of you before the dust
Drives the fields to weeds and the corn leans
In the heat of the sun.

                    I have cursed the sweat,
As you remember well, but still the hoe,
Smoothly worn, has been the friend
No man could ever be. This you
Will understand: for you have known, have gripped
Its power in your hand and fought the muscled earth,
The bugs and even God to get a crop
Grown and into town, have known the hoe
Pressing against the child that did not live
To grow. But then there were the two and empty fields
Or empty womb is not the blinding pain
When two can curse and share the burden of
The contagious hearse that not only
Broke the purse but broke the thing
Between one man and his woman. But this
Does seem unfair: you were more than mere woman.
And now? I wonder how many worms
You are, or if I have split your seed

And left you open to the sun, the calm
Indifference of the quiet moon,
Or the hungry bellies of the stupid birds
That flock and black the fields, determined
To see ruin spread and bake the fields and crack
The river beds. You always said to pray
For prayer would overflow the water well
And turn the stone to bread, but I...but we
Have broken teeth on stone and prayer puts a thought
In a fellow's head and drives worry from his tongue
To just behind the ear. I have prayed for a thousand rains,
And I prayed for you: the rain seldom came...

II.

In the morning I will go to the fields after
The hay has shakened the thick dews, after
The horses are watered and the cows walked to
The high green pasture on the east hills.
With a jug of ginger-beer, some cold beef
And bread, and a bag full of strawberries all swinging
In a bucket on my arm, I will ride
The roan mare to the north lot and see
If I can't mow ten square acres before
The sun has leapt too high and uncontrollable
In the sky.

When I just can't take any more sun,
And sweat, and god-damned flies I'll hunt out your
Cedar by the pile of stones and just ease-off
For and hour and let the sun and bugs
Play all the havoc they think necessary
To finish out their day's chores. When
The berries are gone and the beer is flat and I
Have had myself some little nap and the sun

Leans toward the big red barn then I will lead
The mare back to harness and lead myself
Back to the high seat of the old mower
Where I can play king for an hour, a king
Who can stretch his glance and see as far as he owns,
As far as the stream rolling down "Witches Hill"
And through the rumpled fields of daisies, clover and rye.
And when my eye is worn-out from staring
And the mare, shaking her mane, is restless to go,
Then I again will mow and I suppose,
Thank God (or whoever it is that spits
The seeds of rain into the earth and pulls
Up the hay and the grain like a robin
Pulling the tail of a worm), will thank this God
For the strength of my arm and the power of the mare,
And the rain and wretched heat of the sun, and thank
Whoever God is for the hands that hold
The reins and lower the blade and make sure
It's hay that's cut. Yesterday the blade
Sawed off, neat as you can, the grey head
Of a mouse trying to break an autumn nut
That winter spared. I felt a drop of blood,
Warm and shy, hiss against my cheek.

So all morning long and all afternoon
I'll mow, stopping now and then to give
My horse a rest, and we will work together
Until I see the first bat rise
And streak against the sky.

                    I do not care
To return home and if my horse were not
Tired and if the grazed cows did not
Wait by the locked gate near the barn then I
Would stay within the fields and work all night

By the stars, no matter how dull or how bright.
Home is a house of ghosts and shadows, sounds
Which are restless throughout the long dark night,
Dark even when the moon lies asleep on the pillow.
A man can't take the moonlight in his arms.

The Hawk

For Asa

I rise morning after morning
And walk the wet meadows
Though I never frighten off the hawk
With a gun or with a cry,
But I have sometimes held
It bread and bits of meat
To coax it from the sky.

His talons drip with honey,
His beak is full of gentian leaves
And blossoms, and his eye
Shines with a strange kindness
As his feathers dust the sky.

What drives the babe to suck
And kneads the blood with passion;
What tickles idiots
And has them laugh
Drives my hands to clutch
His feathers and wear
Them in an ancient fashion.

TO LESBIA FROM CATULLUS 1958

A better man could have made your soul,
Your eyes more beautiful;
A better poet...immortal.

CATULLUS TO LESBIA, 1958

Like a sword
Slicing through silk
I explore
The realms of you
Becoming
The possessor
Possessed...
Searching
The dark
Of the flower
I seek
The morning dew.

I AM THE SUN

I Am The Sun

A Song of Praise, Defiance and Determination

> "I did not know then how much was ended. When I look back from this high hill of old age, I can see the butchered women and children lying heaped and scattered along the crooked gulch as plain as when I saw them with eyes still young. And I can see that something else died there, and was buried in the blizzard. A people's dream died there. It was a beautiful dream...the nation's hoop is broken and scattered."
>
> —Black Elk

Father, I come;
Mother, I come;
Brother, I come;
Father, give us the arrows.

Chankpe Opi Wakpala!

Father, I hold one for Big Foot;
Mother, I hold one for Black Coyote;
Brother, I hold one for Yellow Bird;
Father, give us back the arrows.

Chankpe Opi Wakpala!

Father, give us sky;
Father, give us sun in the east;
Father, give us night in the west;
Father, watch our shadows;
Father, give us back our arrows.

Chankpe Opi Wakpala!

Mother, your breast is bare;
Mother, your breast was not enough to sustain us;
Mother, hold our bones now;
Mother, we search for our arrows.

Chankpe Opi Wakpala!

Brother, we cried for you;
Brother, we called you back;
Brother, we descended with you.
      and your flesh
      and your bones
      and your fur which kept us warm;
Brother, when our arrows are returned
      we will seek you.

Chankpe Opi Wakpala!

Arrows, now the skies are diseased;
Arrows, now the earth is diseased;
Arrows, now the people are sick on dreams;
Arrows, come back to us.

Chankpe Opi Wakpala!

Our father is gone;
Our father has fled;
Our father has turned his face;
Arrows, give us back our father.

Our mother has closed her eyes;
Our mother has closed her mouth;
Our mother had closed her heart;
Arrows, give us back our mother

Our brother has wandered away;
Our brother does not walk;
Our brother has gone down;
Arrows, give us back our brother.

The arrows broke at Greasy Grass;
The arrows broke with Crazy Horse;
The arrows broke with Sitting Bull;
Father, give us back our arrows.

Chankpe Opi Wakpala!

In the river of his blood,
    I stand in Bigfoot's grave;
In the shout of fear,
    I shout for Black Coyote;
In the dance of his dream,
    I dance for Yellow Bird;
Father, give us back our arrows.

We will put the center back
    in your country;
We will circle stones and make the hoop
    in your country;
We will plant the seed of the sacred tree
    in your country.

We will fill the river with water;
We will fill the woods with trees;
We will clothe the bones with flesh;
We will empty the graves;
We will call back the wolf, the deer;
We will build the walls of the dream;
We will make and tend the fire,
    in your country.

For I am the Sun!

I am the sun!

I stand above the world.

Chankpe Opi Wakpala!
Chankpe Opi Wakpala!

Father give us back our arrows,
       and make a woman into a child,
           a boy into a man,
           a girl into a woman,
           an arrow into a country,
           a country into a home.
           a home into the sun.

Chankpe Opi Wakpala!
Chankpe Opi Wakpala!
Chankpe Opi Wakpala!

Father, give us no more graves;
Father, give us back our arrows!
We have learned to hold them sacred!

I SEE WITH MY OWN EYES

For Pedro Bissonette

> "The maker of this song, while in the spirit world, asks and
> receives from the Father some of the old arrows."
>
> —James Mooney,
> *The Ghost-Dance Religion*
> *and the Sioux Outbreak of 1890*

Give me the arrows.
They have come,
They have come.

Grey lights up the sky,
Earth yawns.

Give me the arrows,
Father, give them to me;

Rivers flow, ribbon
The cottonwood valleys;
Tipis rise against the dawn,
Against the dawn.

They have some;
I shall eat pemmican.

> "At one time, I thought all I could ever be is drunk.
> When I found out I could fight for my people, I became a man."
>
> —Pedro Bissonette

I became a man,
And blood flowed through my fingers;
I stepped on paper flowers,
I walked among wreaths.
Give me arrows!

The herd blazes gold in the morning.
All I
          could ever be
                    ever be
                              is a drunk, is a drunk.
They have come, they have come.
Father, give them to me.

I grunt in his grunt,
And lay off my clothes
So that the hoof
Could trod my flesh.
All I could ever be...
I heard Crazy Horse,
I hear Rain-in-the-Face...
                    ever be.

Deliberate aim...
Brain crushed, breast crushed;
Into the wind-swept dust
Of empty prairie,
The dried river with leafless cottonwoods.
The herd thundered through
The paper flowers of my grave.
Give me arrows!
I found out I could fight for my people.
I found out
          I could fight
                    for my people
                              people!

I went to the mountain,
I went to the Spirit
                    of the sky,
                    of the river.

I stood in the sun...
                    hungry, thirsty...

To await the dream.
The mountain rumbled;
Springs broke open from the rock;
I drank clear water.
Dizzy in the sun dream,
I became a man.
I see with my own eyes.

When I became a man I became a shadow;
When I became a shadow I became a light!

There is a dry river,
A felled cottonwood,
An empty prairie,
An open grave...!
There is a saloon in Tulsa,
A jail in Denver,
A welfare office in Oakland,
A grave in South Dakota.

All I could ever be is a drunk
                    a drunk...!

Now in the lands of the Father,
I call out:
Give me the arrows.
I will place them in hands
Not to avenge blood
But to keep strong hearts;
I will place the arrows in hands
To hold the lodge,
To hold the sacred tree,

To tighten the sacred hoop
Surrounding the holy fire;
And in grey and toothless age
Smile upon the young
As they walk, hungry and thirsty,
In the face of the sun,
In the embrace of the Spirit,
The Father,
To the holy mountain
To have their dreams,
They, who will become men
For the people

Give them the arrows
                     the arrows.

They have come
             they have come.

I see with my own eyes!

NORTH: POEMS OF HOME

First Rule

stones must form a circle first not a wall
open so that it may expand
to take in new grass and hills
tall pines and a river
expand as sun on weeds, an elm, robins;
the prime importance is to circle stones
where footsteps are erased by winds
assured old men and wolves sleep
where children play games
catch snowflakes if they wish;
words cannot be spoken first

as summer turns spring
caterpillars into butterflies
new stones will be found for the circle;
it will ripple out a pool
grown from the touch
of a water spider's wing
words cannot be spoken first

that is the way to start
with stones forming a wide circle
marsh marigolds in bloom
hawks hunting mice
boys climbing hills
to sit under the sun to dream
of eagle wings and antelope;
words cannot be spoken first

GOWANE

For Donna

Geese climbed the moon in the scent of wild grapes;
The great young elms arched in the autumn winds;
Chestnuts and walnuts plummeted to earth in the dark
Of the watchful night. No bird sang, nor wolf howled.
A young man smoked his sumac in the firelight.

In the distance a faint light shone on Hill Island...
The bleached-ones' camp. Flames shot through the night;
The thin tongues whipped through the dark like the tails
Of deer rushing through the thick brush of the woods.

He held watch for the Canarsee this night;
Watched for the bleached-ones to cross the waters
Where shad and sturgeon slept in the quiet of deep shadows.
All night he stood his post, wakeful, showing neither eye
To close in sleep. The foolish strangers who had taken
The tip of Minna-atn, perhaps, were greedy.

He watched for the strangers and he watched for the Mohiks,
The wolf men, who sent their sachems for tribute
Of dried shellfish and shell beads, or the blood of his people.

He watched the geese fly against the moon
And listened to the deer's hushed tread;
He thought of the berries the women would pick in the meadows,
He thought of the elk the men hunted, he thought of the bear
That roamed his country. He watched for the strangers,
And wondered if they would stay in his land Menachawik.

At dawn the camp dogs came, and young girls for water;

His headman came, and spoke of his deed: the steady watch
Of the night. He announced to the village that henceforth
This young man would be called by the name Gowane
For he had kept the night's vigil, the village safe
From attack at the place of little sleep.
He proved the watchful one. Now he could go to his round house
And once there he found his wife had a pot of hot fish soup
And his deerskins warm and ready to receive him.

After eating, he rolled into the comfortable skins.
He felt proud and good in his strong heart
For he had been named Gowane, one of little sleep.
He had stood night sentry at the watchful place, Gowanus.

Fish swam nearby in the waters and a bear stood straight
To reach the high spray of the blackberry bush.
Again for another day the village was safe.

COLD CREEK

trout speckled in April dawn
slivered with silver of early spring...
song poured to the willows of daylight
over the sandy banks of the creek
cold to the toe, cold to the boy
caught like rainbow trout
by the hook in the jaw;
song poured to the grass, minnows
burnished in the leaping of noon
over and down the hills, quarried
and crushed in the fist of the pimple
that would claim me to manhood,
manhood shied like rats
in the haybarn seeking blood
not the hen's eggs mama said;
song poured to the flowing creek,
jumping rocks, staggering down dams,
thrusting weight against stones;
song poured to the winds
that bristled my cowlicks and burnt
goosepimples into the flesh of my thighs;
song poured into the night willows
with only shadows under

then words crept out like mice in the dark,
and Cold Creek, that had leaped from a hill
a spring, turned and entered the wide river
with my song

HOME

for Rick

North
> north by the star
hills under, cows, brush
river broken by spring
men broken by harvest and stone
fields and fields of stone
stone tall as a boy
boys tall as crab apple
spruce weighted with moonshine

north
> north by the star
starlight that parts the corn
starlight that glimmers on autumn
squash and beans
apples caught by the frost
frosty women hanging clothes
balloon in the tight sharp air
pine-stove melts those figures, fingers

north
> north by the star
old men smoke in a circle
north by the village
men smoke in a circle
over the feathers of a partridge
that drummed on the floor of the forest
deviled in the ambush of the wind

north
      north by the star
we go home, we go...
to the pheasant, woodchuck, muskrat
the last deer standing the summer
of flies on the blood of the wolf
howled in the north
           north by the star
starring the Adirondacks
forgotten in the rush for campsites
brown bear mussled to honey-
cookies tourist tease
to the crackling of their arms
and the butchery of the bear
who will not share the berry picking
with the girls of June this year
in the north, north
      by the north star
hills under, brush, cabins, towns
rivers broken by spring

we go home to the north
        north by the star

MULLEINS ARE MY ARMS

mulleins are my arms
and chicory
the sinew of my flesh;
May strawberries
are the blood of my legs
and the sun of summer;
maples are my head
and sugar the sap of my tongue
that runs in the warm wind;
crocus are my eyes;
turtle the feet of my winter

seasons are a rumble of
herded old cows
coming to barn from pastures
before snow covers corn,
and the mare jumps the fence
crazy from glittering stones

marvelous is the miracle of spring
and, also, the weight of winter;
the plum which ripens,
drops seeds into pockets of earth
vacated by gophers;
the rabbits that sleep,
and the bear

incredible is the force of April,
and the lust of January;
in the summer of the second year
mulleins grow another branch,

chicory spreads to another field

LAND

1976

Torn, tattered, yet rugged
in the quick incline of bouldered hills
crab appled, cragged, lightning-struck birch, cedar;
wilderness muzzled; forests—kitchen tables and bedposts
of foreign centuries; meadows cowed
beyond redemption, endurance, violated
by emigres' feet, and vineyards alien
to indigenous squash and berry,
fragile lupine and iris of the pond;
while wounded willows bend in the snow
blown north by the west wind

1820

spring lifts under drifts, saplings
hold to the breeze, larks sing, strawberries
crawl from under snow, woodchucks run
stone walls of new cemeteries and orchards;
apples blossom, thistle bloom

(Madame de Feriet's ghost prowls the miraged bridge
spanning Black River and her mansion lanterns
glow in the clear darkness of the French dream,
hazeled in the richness of her opulence

the lands she would hold out to tenants for rent
have neither clearings nor plows;
the disillusionment lorried her trunks to France,
her mansion to ashes, her bridge to dust in 1871,
her savings to pittance, her dream to agony

Madame de Feriet gave her French aristocratic manner
to a signpost at the edge of the county road,
tangled now by yellow roses and purple vetch)

1976

April lifts from under the drifts of grey
snow piled by plows ruthless in their industrial
might to free roads and make passage
for trucks and automobiles to hurry to the grave
with dead horses in the far pasture
that no longer sustains the hunger of bleating lambs

virgin spring lifts, its muddy face scarred
and mapped with trails of progress, its smoke
rising in pine, maple, flowering aspen,
chicory weed and clods, manure of waste, whey,
abandoned farm houses and barns shaking in the wind...
blind old men caught without canes in the storm;
spring bloody in its virginity, its flow corrupted,
raped in zoned courts of law that struck quarried hills...
a great god's lance thrust in the quickness of electric sun

rage of spring rivers, swollen with anger...
cold voice growling through the night...swirling,
swallowing the soft shoulders of shoreline;
the rage of the aged shackled to history
and the crumbling bones of its frame, fisted against
the night, shaking the cane against the dark, the bats
fluttering in the balmy summer eve, fireflies creeping
through the young green grass of the long fresh meadows

1812

the north, the north aches in the bones, the land,

in the elms' limbs gently singing in that August
breeze, bereft of holiday and festival, ghost and voice...
tunneled by gophers; ticks and fleas stuck to an old dog's back

(General Brown marched his men to Sacketts Harbor,
struck the British in the red belly
and went home to lift a pint to his deeds
and captured acres, to ville a town, erect a fence)

1976

the gooseberry is diseased, and the elm,
stone walls broken, sky cracked, pheasants
and young muskrats sterilized, and fields

DANCING BACK STRONG THE NATION

LISTEN, THE OLD WOMAN CAME HERE

"Looking back...I will know."
—Karoniaktatie

Listen...
The old woman
               came here
          she brought seeds
                    in her fingernails
          she brought wind
          she brought children
The old woman
               came here
          we came here

I WENT NORTH

I went north in winter
        they were dancing in the Longhouse
        women danced
        old men danced
        children danced
We ate cornbread

I went north in winter
        heard wolf
        heard a child cry
        heard the drum
I knew they would dance back strong the Nation

I went north

DRUMS

listen...

drums drum
        dance dance
rattles rattle
        sing sing
drums dance
rattles sing
pause and
        dance and

drums drum
to the song
        of the young
                        warriors

listen...

thunder thunder
                shakes
thunder shakes the floor

The Women

east west
west east
east west
east west

women women
            move move
east west
            move move

We come to greet
We come to greet and thank
                      the women
      hands gnarled in sweetgrass
      hands worn with corn meal
      hands wet with babies
            move move
            east west

We come to greet and thank the women

DANCE

listen...
a hundred feet
a hundred feet
         move move
         move move
from the ancients
into Grandfather's shoes
         move move
         a hundred feet
         move move

We come
We come to greet
We come to greet and thank
     the strawberry plants
          growing
          growing there
          as tall
          as tall as high
          as tall as high grasses
               grasses

     mice in the grass
     chicory in the fields
     owl on a branch

We come
We come to greet and thank
We come
     to dance

MOCCASIN

Listen...

moccasin moccasin
                circle circle
                dance dance

drums drum
        pound pound
rattles rattle
        sing sing

wind howls like a wolf on the hill

thunders thunder
                shake shake

wind sings in the cold air

moccasin moccasin
                move move

wind howls
wind sings
                leaves fall in the frost
                apples ripen in the frost
                wolves seek lairs in the frost
                snow falls
                hills rise
                sun sets
                        sun sun
                                sets

moccasin moccasin

circle circle
dance dance

We come to greet and thank
the winds
the birds
the snow
the drum
the drummer
the dance
the dancer
move move
sun move
moccasin

GOING HOME

The book lay unread in my lap
snow gathered at the window
from Brooklyn it was a long ride
the Greyhound followed the plow
from Syracuse to Watertown
to country cheese and maples
tired rivers and closed paper mills
home to gossipy aunts...
their dandelions and pregnant cats...
home to cedars and fields of boulders
cold graves under willow and pine
home from Brooklyn to the reservation
that was not home
to songs I could not sing
to dances I could not dance
from Brooklyn bars and ghetto rats
to steaming horses stomping frozen earth
barns and privies lost in blizzards
home to a Nation, Mohawk
to faces I did not know
and hands which did not recognize me
to names and doors
my father shut

THE STEELWORKER

For Peter

In the hot Brooklyn night we stood
at a bar drinking beer, and he said,

> "Riding the sky on steel girders
> solid under my feet, wind balances;
> beer tastes good after work
> in these neighborhood bars on Nevins St.,
> but with all the big wages
> there is nothing to pray to
> here in the Brooklyn ghetto
> where my kids don't know
> if they're Black or Puerto Rican;
> too many bars on Nevins St., too many beers
> make me dizzy; I forget to sing
> and will slip one noon
> from those high steel girders."

And he took hold the shadowed hands
of Wolf and Bear and Turtle.

LEGACY

my face is grass
          color of April rain;
arms, legs are the limbs
          of birch, cedar;
my thoughts are winds
          which blow;
pictures in my mind
          are the climb uphill
          to dream in the sun;
hawk feathers, and quills
of porcupine running
the edge of the stream
which reflects stories
of my many mornings
and the dark faces of night
mingled with victories
of dawn and tomorrow;
corn of the fields and squash...
the daughters of my mother
who collect honey
and all the fruits;
meadow and sky are the end of my day
          the stretch of my night
yet the birth of my dust;
my wind is the breath of a fawn
the cry of the cub
the trot of the wolf
whose print covers
the tracks of my feet;
my word, my word,
loaned
legacy, the obligation I hand
to the blood of my flesh

the sinew of the loins
to hold to the sun
and the moon
which direct the river
that carries my song
and the beat of the drum
to the fires of the village
which endures.

YAIKINI
Strawberry Moon

a fierce serpent's tail
lies across my legs;
its mouth breathes into my mouth
when elms were sweet
      squash tasted of sun
      corn grew in circles
      outside the village
      near streams where trout
dove through air for spiders
and cedar scented afternoon
it has lain upon my back
under the west wind...
muskrat in its jaw...
more days than needles
on the tamarack
sweetgrass is for weaving
and summer berries
for a child's tongue
(eagles soared, wolves
trotted mountain slopes)
a youth will come
and his arrow
will rid my spine of this serpent

...

together we will watch
it quiver in the falling dusk
      morning turtle eyes the east
      smoke rises from a house
      though snow covers pine
      the roots are deep

and will survive winter
the serpent will return to the sea
and though it leaves a fang mark
on my throat it will fade
　　　　bear awakens
　　　　to the smell of crocus;
　　　　it is the time for bathing
　　　　and then for planting
　　　　and for a good smoke by the fire
...

　　　　I will talk with the old people
　　　　and come May seek the early thistle
　　　　and sweet strawberry
and be healed

In My Sixth August

My father wades the morning river
tangled in colors of the dawn.
He drags a net through the cold
waters; he spits tobacco juice,
stumbles. Light warns the minnows
that hide under bullheads. Sharp air
smells of wild lobelia and apple.

In my sixth August a kingfisher
rattles from a willow; I am too
busy picking iris in the wet fields
to know a game warden shakes his head
above us on the narrow bridge to home.
The west wind has trapped our scent
and light prisons our mobile hands.

WILD STRAWBERRY

For Helene

And I rode the Greyhound down to Brooklyn
where I sit now eating woody strawberries
grown on the backs of Mexican farmers
imported from the fields of their hands,
juices without color or sweetness

      my wild blood berries of spring meadows
      sucked by June bees and protected by hawks
      have stained my face and honeyed
      my tongue...healed the sorrow in my flesh

      vines crawl across the grassy floor
      of the north, scatter to the world
      seeking the light of the sun and innocent
      tap of the rain to feed the roots
      and bud small white flowers that in June
      will burst fruit and announce spring
      when wolf will drop winter fur
      and wrens will break the egg

      my blood, blood berries that brought laughter
      and the ache in the stooped back that vied
      with dandelions for the plucking,
      and the wines nourished our youth and heralded
      iris, corn and summer melon

      we fought bluebirds for the seeds
      armed against garter snakes, field mice;
      won the battle with the burning sun
      which blinded our eyes and froze our hands
      to the vines and the earth where knees knelt

and we laughed in the morning dew like worms
and grubs; we scented age and wisdom

my mother wrapped the wounds of the world
with a sassafras poultice and we ate
wild berries with their juices running
down the roots of our mouths and our joy

I sat here in Brooklyn eating Mexican
berries which I did not pick, nor do
I know the hands which did, nor their stories...
January snow falls, listen...

FAYE

wind calls a flute in the pine
wind drums in the needles

a girl waits for a boy
who will come

the girl waits
for the boy

with a mug of sweet tea
and a far gaze;

snow fills the woods
as the girl waits

for the boy
while the pine fire

in the pot-belly stove
warms a dog too old for rabbits

In the Flow

For Bro. Benet

I learn water
      in the sky
clouds surface
      over sycamores
minnows nibble
      a drowned butterfly

I learn rivers
      by sitting still
watch the crevice
      of my brow
hear wind ripple
      break reflections

I learn water
      in the summer
fox trek down to drink
      autumn whispers

Eye catches
      the hawk
in the winter
      sky

ONLY AS FAR AS BROOKLYN

BOYS
(Vision)

the hawk flew
to the crazy mountain
plums grew large and red
stained hands and teeth

the crazy mountain shivered
smoke rose from the rocks
the crazy mountain moved,
called hawk, hawk
catch me in your talons

red plums fell to the grass
the hawk told me to go home
they told me I had dreamed
on the crazy mountain
in the time of falling plums

hawk,
I must remember this story
to tell the young boys
fishing in the creek

I SHALL NOT WRITE OF LOVE

morning's bare shore;
sea plums have no flesh

    I shall marry
    grow cruel with winter,
    dry crisp like chicory
    that hangs above the fire

cats never leave the apartment;
the maid comes on Monday;
the library's usually open

    not that I can't
    but I shall marry

hung over from all that
I bolt the door to intrusions
that peck on windows

    for a while
    if I can resist
    for a while

I shall not write of love.

WINKTE*

*"He told me that if nature puts a burden on a man by
making him different, it also gives him a power...'*
—John (Fire) Lame Deer,
Sioux Medicine Man

We are special to the Sioux!
They gave us respect for strange powers
Of looking into the sun, the night.
They paid us with horses not derision.

To the Cheyenne we were no curiosity.
We were friends or wives of brave warriors
Who hunted for our cooking pots,
Who protected our tipis from Pawnee.

We went to the mountain for our puberty vision.
No horse or lance or thunderbird
Crossed the dreaming eye which would have sent us
Into war or the hunter's lonely woods.
To some song floated on the mountain air,
To others colors and design appeared on clouds,
To a few words fell from the eagle's wing,
And they took to the medicine tent,
And in their holiness made power
For the people of the Cheyenne nation.
There was space for us in the village.

The Crow and Ponca offered deerskin
When the decision to avoid the warpath was made.
And we were accepted into the fur robes
Of a young warrior, and lay by his flesh
And knew his mouth and warm groin;
Or we married (a second wife) the chief,

83 ✳

And if we fulfilled our duties, he smiled
And gave us his grandchildren to care for.

We were special to the Sioux, Cheyenne, Ponca
And the Crow who valued our worth and did not spit
Names at our lifted skirts nor kick our nakedness.
We had power with the people!

And if we cared to carry the lance, or dance
Over enemy scalps and take buffalo,
Then that, too, was good for the Nation.
And contrary to our stand we walked backwards.

*Sioux word for male homosexual

PAPAGO I

Down into the centuries of your breath
        my centuries prodded

        I meant to leave a song on your ear,
        rabbit fur, a cup of corn,
        a plume, a bowl of apples and warm wind.
        ...
        I meant to leave my name whispered
        on your mouth because secrets
        are long between your Arizona rocks
        and my old cedar woods of home.
        ...
        I meant to kindle a campfire
        to warn off wolves which would gnaw
        our bones and carry off our shadows.

Down into the centuries of your blood
        my centuries prodded
unearthed the passions of your veins,
the savage fumblings of my hands
which struck the dawn of your movements
and swept winds through the sunset of my day
breaking sky colors into thin light.

Down into the contours of your flesh
        my flesh prodded
but not without gentleness.

        I meant to leave our names scratched into stone
        that no river could erase, nor wind defile.
        ...
        I meant to leave my arms in your arms
        and take only the gift of your voice

whispering the motions of my blood,
the taut muscles of our race.

PAPAGO II

With these hands
     I touch the bright mirage
     of your ancient earth...

With this mouth
     I open your lips
     to rain...

With this flesh
     I break the rock
     of your painted
     and sacred mountain
     and silence the panther
     in the dark cave
     of your cold breast...

With these words
     I bind the wound
     and close the scar
     across the Arizona deserts
     of your tribal home...

With these words
     I seal an hour
     and sew the rent
     which I might
     have torn...

After Reading the Greek Poet

For Larry

Cavafy, your young man
with quiet eyes and honey skin
walks along the river
wagging a finger at older men
then enters the house flushed,
and exits, later, pale and worn
from too many kisses
as the lover raises the window shade
and his dark eyes watch him as he goes.

COMANCHE OF THE YAMAHA

sunned to day
Yamaha
scratched the desert;
mooned to night
Yamaha
grunted the mountains
cold in the river of darkness...
frost rimming goggles
air tearing under the helmet
to scream within the ear

Comanche scout feathered and painted
eager to war Oakland
hotels and smoky barrooms
eager to strike coup
on some head
who kneels to the lance
and the touch of soft Comanche hands

the cactus flowers
mountains erupt in volcanic passion
rivers and air run wild
Yamaha, mooned and sunned,
screeched to a braked halt
and the Comanche slid
in the saddle to paradise

KODACHROME DOUBLE EXPOSURE

The boy lies quietly among the grasses;
An empty blouse pillows his head;
Garish green sunlight floats and filters
Across and through his yellow spiked thighs
And blue-green grass has nailed the thin arms
And chest to the prune-colored earth;
Gauzy light washes his brittle lips.
Blades of grass, woven into texture of skin.
Intricately woven like needles into muscles
Of arm, belly, buttock, compressed cheek
Skewered into the grassy sky and blue ground
Cover the opaque body from the long
Singular line of ants approaching.

KNEADING THE BLOOD

STRAWBERRYING

morning
broods
        in the wide river
Mama bends
        light
        bleeds
        always
in her days of
        picking
(our fields are stained)

the moon, bats
        tell us
        to go
in the scent of
        berries

fox
        awaken
                in stars

THE PARTS WE KEEP

In memory of William Mothersell
d. August, 1976

we dropped you into dust
    amongst marigolds

we fed you to April trout
    grass growing in your field

we gave parts to perch, bass
    and moose of north Canada
    the autumn fawn you left
    in alder and hickory woods
    the black rivers of Coleman lanterns
    the winter plow of muscle

we kept you from death
    of bones and sinew
    kept your nails and hair strong
    teeth from falling off the jaw
    gave away beagles, rifles
    rusty muskrat traps

we listen to the wild goose honk;
    you trudge maple, birch
    run the hounds

and we went home to drink
    your laughter in a glass
    or two of whiskey
    an epitaph, an anecdote

there is beauty in death

we insult your nerves
　　　　by grasping them together
　　　　and claiming them tendons of the man
　　　　parts of the human being,
　　　　and in reverse separate
　　　　the joints from the body
　　　　the voice from the tongue

eulogies are usually lies and myths
　　　　fitted together by priests
　　　　trying to pass the dead
　　　　to God, exhorting nature
　　　　decorating flesh and soul

we will not lie
　　　　you were nothing more
　　　　than your colds and fevers
　　　　your fishpoles and guns
　　　　your worn hunting socks and boots
　　　　your grandson's nose

we barely knew the ticking of your clock
　　　　the weather of your dreams
　　　　the smell of your curse
　　　　the taint of your sin
　　　　nor touched the warmth of your blood
　　　　as you welcomed neighbors to supper
　　　　in-laws to bed

we will not legend you into heaven
　　　　nor mock your prayer which raised
　　　　an orange marigold
　　　　and blessed the fawn
　　　　or eel swimming in dark waters...
　　　　saying, we come again

come again

for a man's history is a record,
a diary not the wish fulfillments
of a broken wife, or son
the hope of the fatherless daughter

there is a miracle in death

we dug the grave
           brought roses and pompoms
           mass was said, the high holy mass
           and the priest dropped absolution
           on the metal of your coffin
           six friends nailed it tight
           and carried your weight into darkness;
           your steel box denies you to eternity
           and the commingling of your dust
           with the marigolds of your garden
           and the blood
           of your sire and grandson

we can only kneel at the headstone
           not hear your curse on the wind
           nor taste you on the hawk
           nor catch you on the hook
           nor scent you on the trillium
           all your parts have been sealed
           we have only
           the roar of your automobile
           the feel of a handshake

there is a creation in death
           we have no part

BOSTON TEA PARTY

BOSTON TEA PARTY

1. Assigned

A.

Night closed as the door exposed candles
in little red jars scattered
about the room smelling of boiling tea,
a special tea of licorice and sassafras.

His hair was festooned with birds,
their songs silenced in the loose strands
weeping down the naked flesh of his back.
Birds hung at his waist
in folds and flow of Polynesian fabric,
purple of the sea, green of the mountain.
Kittens played with twine
balled and fisted on the belly of the floor.

Ship-rolled I moved into the light,
face reddened but altar-calm, took a chair
especially arranged with the only cushion,
and held the mug of enigmatic tea
terrifying in its ambivalence.
What realms would I travel from that brew?
What new worlds discover?
What birds would alight on the hair?
Would snakes peel from the mouth;
would fingers extend into lizard tails;
tongue become an angel of flight?

Tall as a priest or goddess he radiated smiles
over the late hours of the night.
He washed my feet, bathed loins,

presed his mouth to the spirit
he thought he touched in the soul, memory.
He blew feathers on my ribs,
danced drums on my naked knees, cheekbones;
blessed prayers upon my eyelids.

The night was holy, time late.
Mystery shuddered as he knelt before me
as though asking my hands to bless his life,
confirm my secret powers.

He conjured buffaloes from my feet, armpits.
Rattles banged and shook from my teeth.
An elk reared from the floor,
floated through the glass of the dark window.
Hawks fluttered from my ears to the cracked
ceiling, a chalice trembling as wine
spilled down wretched walls of his heart splitting
in the light of those red votive candles lit
to strike the spirit of my history,
ancestry, my drums and rattles,
my curdling war cry, a bloody scalp raised
in my hands to the triumph of the night,
my face black with victory, the slain spirit
resting a pulsing liver between my teeth.
I was savior and warrior, priest and poet,
fertile and fallow, savage and prophet,
angel of death and apostle of truth.
I was the messenger of gods and demons.
He knew my powers could fathom
the darkness of the light.
I bed in Salem.

His ribs opened for my arrow;
his head split for the tomahawk, the club;

his pain longed for my hands to touch it,
soothe it, mold it into a receptacle, an urn
of blood and ashes stirred with a prayer stick
while my chants chewed the potions
that fettered his brain and soul.

I'd drink his tea and spit out rocks.
I'd suck flesh and spit out frogs.
I would paint kingfishers on his thighs,
deer on his heels, morning glories on his brow.
I would heat stones and steam off sin.
I would tear fifty pieces of flesh
to feed hummingbirds, and marry his dry bones
with Satan and they would live forever
on my fingertips, an apple bough.

Was I not touching the universe—
a feather in my hair, bells on my ankles?
Was I not master of dark dealings of dryads?
I was to raise the pipe, smoke, allow the puffs
to bathe his priesthood which he would gladly loan to me,
naming me the high priest of his foolish
pagan altar adorned with plastic geraniums and peacock feathers.

Pity the unanointed, the damned.
Absolve the guilty and the hangman.

B.

I switched on the bathroom light...
it broke the room crawling with roaches.
A canary hung dead in his greasy hair;
his flesh was caked with yellow powder;
his earlobes etched with butterfly wings.
"Turn off the light." His pain pleaded.

The candles were dipped in cats' blood.
My severed spirit had been the sacrifice.
He kissed my ring at the door
with the moon down and the cymbals silent.

C.

Boston winds pushed me into dawn,
Dogwoods bloomed a street, empty and grey.
The Charles was clean, beautiful
in the morning calm. A boy
rode by on a bicycle, his blond hair
blowing free in the breeze. I was damp
with sweat and dew and could hear
the Transit grumble under my feet.
Aging bones ached, a little arthritic,
I would suppose, probably.
Potassium would help the numbing pain
and a ball to roll in the fist
would keep fingers
limp from rage and the kinks of age
in a world estranged from reality.
I picked a crocus. Its scent was fragile.
An ambulance raced past, a dog gnawed a bone.
I crossed the Charles into the grubby
Boston Common to stare at the swan boats,
consult the aging statues whitened by pigeon dung.

2. Radio Interview

He offered me a glass of holy water
to pacify my hunger, request
for a single cup of black coffee...
not allowed in the sanctified confines

where only the smoke of incense curled
from the bowl of Buddha's belly.

Into the microphone he prodded voices
of black witches, magic of an alchemist,
the mystery of a grey guru lean on power
but puffed on adoration.
Gently he questioned my frozen soul.
I revealed only the colors of the day:
forsythia bloomed his April yard,
magnolias striking purple against
the Cambridge sky; the mutability
of the State, its saccharine lies.
I revealed the dirt between my toes,
lice crawling my crotch, wax building
in my ears.
Again I spoke of hunger:
a "Big Mac" would do, instant coffee,
plastic pizza, anything but holy water.

No light hung over my monk's shaped head.
No priest hid behind my coat. He smiled.
At the door he took my hand, pulled my frame
to his, whispered: "I have pain
in my throat. Can you heal the hurt?"
I offered to go home and burn sage.
I had a large can I bought once at the A&P.

Back in Brooklyn listening to the bells
of the Korean Church and the Clark Street
transistors booming our their Sunday Mass
to pigeons and shopping-bag women,
I turned on TV and watched the Marx Brothers
cavort in the old farce, *Horse Feathers*.

May 6, 1980

103 ✳

THE SMELL OF SLAUGHTER

SACRIFICE

For Joe & Carol

wolf tracks
on the snow

I follow between
tamarack and birch

cross the frozen creek
dried mulleins
with broken arms
stand in shadows

tracks move uphill
deeper into snowed conifers

I hurry to catch up
with his hunger

cedar sing in the night
of the Adirondacks
he huddles under bent
red willow
panting

I strip in the cold
wait for him to approach
he has returned
to the mountains

partridge drum
in the moonlight
under black spruce

BOYHOOD COUNTRY CREEK

curved,
changed
by wind
mostly
with hands
and light machinery

rabbits,
muskrats
abandoned cattails
and the smell
of slaughter

mallards,
rainbow trout
speckle
only the memory

bank,
red willow
gave the sandy earth
to a parking lot

voices,
daydreams
merge
into reflection

the air of water
the breath of soil
the sheen of iris
blotted,
the blood
of the hunted

They Tell Me I Am Lost

For Lance Henson

my feet are elms, roots in the earth
my heart is the hawk
my thought the arrow that rides
      the wind across the valley
my spirit eats with eagles on the mountain crag
      and clashes with the thunder
the grass is the breath of my flesh
      and the deer is the bone of my child
my toes dance on the drum
      in the light of the eyes of the old turtle

my chant is the wind
my chant is the muskrat
my chant is the seed
my chant is the tadpole
my chant is the grandfather
      and his many grandchildren
      sired in the frost of March
      and the summer noon of brown August
my chant is the field that turns with the sun
      and feeds the mice
      and the bear red berries and honey
my chant is the river
      that quenches the thirst of the sun
my chant is the woman who bore me
      and my blood and my flesh of tomorrow
my chant is the herb that heals
      and the moon that moves the tide
      and the wind that cleans the earth
      of old bones singing in the morning dust
my chant is the rabbit, skunk, heron

my chant is the red willow, the clay
      and the great pine that bulges the woods
      and the axe that fells the birch
      and the hand that breaks the corn from the stalk
      and waters the squash and catches stars
my chant is a blessing to the trout, beaver
      and a blessing to the young pheasant
      that warms my winter
my chant is the wolf in the dark
my chant is the crow flying against the sun
my chant is the sun
      sleeping on the back of the grass
      in marriage
my chant is the sun
      while there is sun I cannot be lost
my chant is the quaking of the earth
      angry and bold

though I hide in the thick forest
      or the deep pool of the slow river
though I hide in a shack, a prison
though I hide in a word, a law
though I hide in a glass of beer
      or high on steel girders over the city
      or in the slums of that city
though I hide in a mallard feather
      or the petals of the milkwort
      or a story told by my father

though there are eyes that do not see me
      and ears that do not hear my drum
      or hands that do not feel my wind
      and tongues which do not taste my blood

I am the shadow on the field
      the rain on the rock
      the snow on the wind
      the footprint on the water
      the vetch on the grave
I am the sweat on the boy
      the smile on the woman
      the paint on the man
I am the singer of songs
      and the hunter of fox
I am the glare on the sun
      the frost on the fruit
      the notch on the cedar
I am the foot on the golden snake
I am the foot on the silver snake
I am the tongue of the wind
      and the nourishment of grubs
I am the claw and the hoof and the shell
I am the stalk and the bloom and the pollen
I am the boulder on the rim of the hill
I am the sun and the moon
      the light and the dark
I am the shadow on the field

I am the string, the bow and the arrow

In Country Light

Flesh tones streak the blue of frostbite;
cedar sky wheels, hawk over
expanse of salmon afternoon

a child cried because her mother
fell and broke a spider-arm
on river ice

shadows move, deer go;
close the door and stay by the fire;
listen, pinecones crackle
smell supper on the stove

OH, WENDY, ARTHUR

One more night my blood
keeps sleep from the hard pillow.
Sula purrs at the foot of the bed
trying to sing me into dreams.
It doesn't work any more
than warm milk, valium, or exhaustion.
I sit here attempting poems
and fantasizing tours around the world,
wanting to feel your words,
desperate to talk, to tell
how spring climbed up with dawn
and iris bloomed the ridge of my arm,
and we three walked blackberry brambles
balancing on railroad tracks
through blue meadows. Could it be
that sleep defies some drift of happiness
that I can't measure, pin, explicate,
nor file away or the days when that sun
doesn't rise with wildflowers on my cheek.

This particular case of insomnia almost
feels good, knowing you'll soon be here.

Spring 1981

113 ✳

HORSES

The red horses romp
the windy green
disappearing
an echoed scream
into the fires
of the agonized sun
but the bronzed horses
return purely white
the hoofs pounding
the turf of twilight
into the blue horses of night
they charge the range
and come riderless black
riderless the horses come

BLACKROBE: ISAAC JOGUES

PEACEMAKER

mountains bristle
with long needles

snow falls

I bring the fire people
this great white pine
to plant and nourish

Atotarho,
you will keep the fire
and care for this pine

Look! an eagle
has alighted
on the spire

mountains have come
to your valley

the down of the thistle
will blanket the earth
beneath the white pine

it will be your couch

Atotarho,
shake the snakes
from your hair

we are one in a circle

AIIONWATHA
(b. circa 1400)

I have listened
and I will aid the stutterer
to unite the people
of this river country.
I will start with the Mohawk,
carry the word to Atotarho of the Onondaga,
advise him to take the bones
from the pot and water the pine.

I will travel and tell this
to both the younger brothers
and the elder brothers.
I will show them
the white roots of peace
as he has instructed.
We will mold a Nation.

Rouen, France

Madame! I go to New France.
The boat leaves tomorrow from Dieppe, the 2nd
Sunday after Easter. We dock
at Quebec. You do not know
how happy I am to learn that now
I will have the opportunity
of saving those lost souls for God.
Bless me and pray for me.
Thank you for the tin of tea.
It will be a comfort in the wilds.
Your very humble son, Isaac Jogues.

AT SEA

Letter to the Father Superior of the Jesuit Order in France

Your High Reverence: I shall
manage this boat! This storm!
This fear! God is in my heart.
I lean upon the staff of Christ.

The sea swells like mountains.
The galley food is inedible.
The crew curses constantly.
Yet, I have few complaints.

God is in my heart,
and He will warm my chill.

The Hurons, *les hures,* I hardly dare
speak of the danger there is
of running oneself amongst
the improprieties of these
savages. I understand adultery
flourishes throughout their country.

Weakness is illness.

I hold to the cross,
Your obedient servant, Isaac Jogues.

LES HURES

Jogues' Journal
Three Rivers

Naked, reddish-brown bodies
glisten like metal in the sunlight;
heavy, barbaric faces
with hooked noses and narrow-
slitted eyes; straight black hair
coiffed with feathers
of brilliant colors...green teal,
royal blue and canary yellow;
faces painted in lightning, color
of thunder; grunt instead of speak;
les hures pluck the hairs of the face.

It is exciting to be
here amongst these fetching
people...rogues we Jesuits
will change into angels and saints.

First Meeting With Kiosaeton

Like some marvelous bird
he stood on the river bank in plumage,
a feather headdress flaming in rainbow colors;
clothed in hide decorated
with beads and porcupine quills.
His neck, his arm hung heavily mailed
with brilliant wampum belts of shells.

He called my by my Huron name, Ondessonk,*
and passed a smoking pipe,
the calumet of peace.
I could not breathe for his resilience;
his air of royalty stunned my sensibilities.
His companions broke into song,
drum beat.
We exchanged gifts of food.

I believe his sincerity.
But what of his warriors
whose faces margin the woods
on which I can discern paint!
What is his power over these men
who would as soon lift my hair
and chop off my thumb
as they would drink my brandy,
smoke our French tobacco.

I will not allow his honeyed words,
his vision or his pipe to halt
my journey south. I
represent the French crown!
and shall not be ambushed by trickery
nor denied my route,

nor fooled by the old man's white paint.

I pray for peace,
and safety,
but my determination
will circumvent all adversity.
I, son of God and priest
of Christ's blood.

Ondessonk: Bird of Prey

KIOSAETON

Ondessonk, through my lips
the Nation speaks. My words
are not malicious.
There is no evil in my heart
for you or your brothers
of the black robe.

My people have many war songs,
but we let them float
in the air as though canoes
drifting down the river.
The ground where we stand
does not pulse from the war dance,
nor does it thirst for your blood.

Here, take some corn and venison.
Eat now, rest. You are in safe
country with my people
who will respect your customs
and invite you into the lodge
if you maintain respect for ours.

CARDINAL RICHELIEU

I sold my own jewels
to build forts at Sainte Marie.
I was impressed with the powerful strength
of the Iroquois. I had visions
of a New France bristling
with industry and commerce,
fur presses breaking, snapping
under the weight of beaver pelts.
My enthusiasm secured grants
from the public treasury, and I
dispatched my own soldiers
to the St. Lawrence to convoy
the Huron traders the full length
of the river. Saints be knighted!
My forces will not be driven out
of the country by Indians.
...I must replace the rings
I've sold in the open market.

APPROACHING THE MOHAWK VILLAGE
Jogues' Journal

I enter the village
my silver cross held upright
though they told me to keep
it hidden in the folds of my robe.

Iroquois, give me your children,
your sick with fever and chill.
I have brought French raisins
to cure your influenza.
I have brought my beads and this cross
to cure your souls. I have
not brought death to your Nation.

Iroquois, give me your chieftains.
Give me your pride and arrogance.
Give me your wildness.
Give me your souls for God
and your sins for hell.

Marginal Note

Richly furred
beaver pelts
hang at the
entrance to
each
lodge.
Ahhhhhhh!

BEAR

What do I want with his raisin!
or his blackrobe, his caul of death.
And those beads or his mumbling.
There is blood on that cross he wears
around his neck, and even though the sun
strikes it and the moon glimmers
from its metal it has a power of
destruction. The beads are
the spittle of a snake. Didn't he come
from Huron country. His piety
is sickening. A weakling. His eye
is always either on pelts or dis-
tracted by the boys. What kind
of human is this who does not hunt
for his own food, but takes if from an old
woman's hand.
                    If he would leave
the children alone...children make men...
I would not interfere with his
breathing.
                    Kwa-ah! Kwa-ah! I'll wail
sadly across this village and send
a runner to Atotarho. He will know what
to do with this blackrobe devil
when he raises that cross to the moon.

There is something strange in his step.

AMONG THE MOHAWKS

Madame! At last! I'm in the village.
There is some fever here. Thankful to God
I have enough raisins. One woman has become
my friend, adopted me as a nephew. She will
protect me as I have enemies in the village.
Already she has freely given me food:
corn soup, dried venison...jerky they call it.
I can rest now awhile and pray.

Ambassador to the Mohawks!
A grand title for one so humble,
Madame will agree. I bring peace
to the breasts of these wildies.

Many beaver in the streams. The pelts
will make handsome chapeaux for our French
gentlemen and the grandees of China.
Salmon are fat. Game plentiful.
They seem to enjoy our brandy.
Your humble son, Isaac Jogues.

THE PEOPLE OF THE FLINT

I openly refute their foolish tales
that the world was built on a turtle's back.
I try to reason the sun possesses no intelligence,
and that the sun is no god to man nor moose...
beautiful that it may be, needful to crops.
I cannot convince them that our Lord
is far more beautiful than this sun they worship.

And the absurd woman who fell from the sky
with the seeds of life under her fingernails,
and who, with the help of some rodent, brought
mud to the turtle's back and created earth with all
things growing...myths, untruths. Gently I shall
dispel this wicked and false belief.

And yet I pity the young children:
the girls picking berries in the long
grasses, the boys readying for war...
children who will not know the peace
of God and His kingdom. I'll persuade
them to the skirts of Mary, virgin mother
of Christ who bore her Son's blood and pain
into miraculous ascension. Isaac Jogues, priest.

WOLF AUNT

I had the right to choose.
It is customary.
My own son was dead.
I needed to replace him
at both the lodge fire
and in my heart.
                Women
need sons not only
for protection and bright
ornaments of quills and feathers.

I adopted Blackrobe...
before the people of the Bear
could strike a tomahawk
into his shaven head.

WOLF AUNT

They came to the lodge door
and called him by name.
Blackrobe, they called.
Blackrobe, come out.

Foolish and determined.
Obstinate, adamant.
Oh! he'll save these children
all right, but from the throne of his god.

I tried to persuade him
to return to the Hurons, his friends.
I told him not to carry that cross
when he walked alone in the village..

holding it, flaunting it in the faces
of both the chiefs and clan mothers.
I told him to stop mumbling
over the sick children,

that the duties of curing
belonged to our doctors
who have centuries of service
and the herbs to heal.

Would he listen! No!
At hearing of an illness
he would drop his bowl of food
and rush out into a blizzard

that cross before him, those beads
clanking on the wind.
I gave his a warm place to sleep,

and deer meat my brother killed.

With my own hands I sewed him moccasins.
I thought he would learn our ways.
All he learned was our language
so he could "speak to the people."

I threatened him
and told him the false-faces
would come when walking
in the woods, they would

bite his flesh and suck
out his spirit. Did he
listen! No, of course not.
Instead he made signs

over me, always smiling what others
thought a smirk, a leer, but he was
smiling. He was too dumb to smirk.
No, not dumb, but foolish.

I was positive that one day the Bear
would grow tired of his posturing,
that some doctor or other would become
jealous, fearful of his powers,

that a clan mother would envy his
living within my lodge,
that some boy would resent his stares,
and that a child would hear his

mumblings and scream out to his
uncle for help. I told him this
every morning of his life

and every night that predicted his death.

And finally they came to the door,
called him by name.
Blackrobe, they called.
Blackrobe, come out!

The moon was very beautiful that night.
Full and yellow. The shadows cast
were long, ominous.
The air was bright, sky blue.

He barely placed his foot on the earth
outside the lodge
when I heard a thump and I knew
his body crumpled under the club.

I will be searching
his bones for years...
bone by bone.

His Visions

One: Revelation

"*Exaudita est oratio tua;*
fiet tibi sicut à me petisti.
Confortare et esto robustus."*

Two: At the Death of Rene Goupil

If I am to die
let it be swift. If I
am to die for Christ
and my heavenly Father, let it be clean.

My aunt says I am foolish.
I should wait for the chiefs' decision,
and that the Seneca
are friendly toward me as well
as the Wolf and Turtle people.
Perhaps!

Rene, and now Jean, my boon companions,
counciled to remain here...one to die
and the other to stay in safety
in the lodge by the fire
where we should be safe. Safe!
Safe from my duty to preach,
to heal, to surrender to God
what is God's. I must accept
the Bear's invitation to the feast.
Now, my only fear is for the life
of young Jean de La Lande who
will perish once my head
rolls on the ground.

What greater sacrifice can I
make for God and the salvation
of these brothers who I shall
and must lead to God.

No, good woman, I will attend the feast.
No, kind Jean, I will respond to the Bear's call.
I will martyr my blood
for the cause of God and even though
I am an alien in this land
I will example my life for Jean
and for these innocents
who are in need of God's love,
Yes, if I am to die let it be swift.

*"Thy prayer is heard. What thou has asked of me is granted thee. Be coura-
geous and steadfast." According to Isaac Jogues, this was the response he
received when he beseeched God to grant him the favor and grace of suffering
for His glory prior to his leaving for his mission among the Hurons.

BEAR

Had he the intelligence
to stay inside the lodge that night
he would still be studying his beads
and waving that cross in the air!
But he was stupid, stupid
in the way of all renegades:
stupid in the way all saints are.
He wanted to be martyred!
He'd sent his communiqués
back to the French in Quebec,
and the Hurons; he'd prayed over
the sick...to the fury of our own
doctors; he mumbled to our children
swathed them with enough fur
to choke out their breath...
he could not bear the sight
of naked flesh, nor two people
coupling in the shadows of the lodge.
Chastity, he called, chastity!
These foreign words
stung many a full-bodied
male and female. Yet, he stared
at the young boys swimming nude
in the river. And flew to make signs
over their heads.
                   It was not so much
that we were sure an army
would follow his step through the woods
—we knew the Frenchmen were
ambitious, and the Dutch conniving
thieves coming from the south—
it was his preaching,
his determined wish to change,

his power to invoke change,
his power to strike out a past
that has taken centuries to build,
and his dark powers culled
from a remote land and godhead
we people feared and mistrusted.

Besides that, I didn't like
the hook of his nose and that cross
he thrust into my teeth and his
whiny breath on my bare arm.
But most his box!

We gave him sanctuary.
We extended all the hospitality
necessary to carry out the law
and to satisfy the demands
of the Seneca. His aunt...hah!
his aunt fed him meat her brother
took down, and squash she labored
hot summers to grow. She picked
him berries and cut sweetgrass
to scent his pillow. She probably
nourished his lust, or gave him
her daughter's loins. (Yet I fear
he abstained, refused that pleasure
while staring at the nude boys playing games.)

The moon was ripe as melons.
Cedar scented the night air.
White pine shimmered in the light.
A hawk had passed over the village
that afternoon, and a snapping
turtle came from the river mud.
There was a smell of parched corn
emanating from a lodge. I told

the men to stay at home
with the women and children.
I told the doctors to prepare
a ceremony, and the soldiers
to sharpen the points of their spears.

With two friends I slipped through
the quiet of the village...not even
the dogs stirred in their lazy sleep.
We approached his aunt's house
and called out to him. I could hear
her arguments...that the Seneca
would come. I knew, however, he would
step out into the darkness.

We spoke briefly, a last
warning for his spirit's flight.
Then the clubs rained upon his head.
Still holding his cross out to us
he sank to the earth, the cross
scraped the flesh of my thigh
and his blood spurted onto my moccasin.

I left my two companions to deal
with his young friend. I
immediately returned to my lodge
and the doctors purged my flesh
with burning cedar smoke, and
awaited the Seneca runners.

I don't know what they did
to his corpse. His old aunt
says she still finds his
bones along the creek bed.
His head was impaled upon
the highest pole of the village stockade.

OCTOBER 18, 1646
Thursday

Madame, I am thirty-nine years old.
My fingers bleed where
old women have chewed the nails.
My feet swell from long hikes
and the snap of dogs' teeth.

They say now that I must
be sacrificed to placate
spirits which have been offended.
The chiefs and the clans
are in council to argue

the will of this Nation.
Spit dries on my cheek.
Madame, your humble son
in Christ and in death,
Isaac Jogues.

THE FRENCH INFORMAL REPORT

We've lost another. With his idiotic
pouch of raisins he went into Mohawk
villages to cure influenza and save
their souls. He was told to wear buckskin,
to be silent, not to raise his cross.

These priests cannot be trusted
to carry out an order.

Oh! he was a good man, pious, devout.
of good cheer, selfless, respected.
That's all true, Ungrudgingly
he tramped the wilds by foot or canoe;
survived privation, torture; overcame
whatever adversity: illness, hunger, lust.

But he was a fool. Should have stayed
in France with the other saints.
He's foiled our plans. The Dutch laugh
in our face, and the English frigates
approach New Amsterdam harbor, their guns
aimed, their greed as large as everyone's.
Beaver is something to squabble about.

Isaac Jogues, get thee to a priory.
Raise turnips within the cloister's walls.
Eat your raisins.
                    The scouting party
found few bones to bury. The Mohawks
are distressed. They dance all night.

TURTLE

They are here now
in blackrobes and hoods;

they walk through the forest
whispering words from a book;

their hair cut short, noses
tight, eyes sharp as a hawk.

One day they will come off the river
with hair as long as our own,

a feather attached loosely,
wearing buckskin shirts

and squash blossom ornaments
about their throats, hanging

on naked chests. You can tell...
some have already begun to smoke

our sumac, bathe, and
speak with the holy men.

One day they will come so thick
we will need to chase them off

with brooms and close the doors
of the lodges as though a pole

stood sentinel at the entrance
and the village was empty.

Someday they will come
to learn...not to teach.

The blackrobes have many feet
beneath their long skirts.

TEKAWITHA (KATERI)

"Lily of the Mohawks"
1656-1680

The hands which hold the silver beads
will never know the hoe, seeds of squash
or beans, or corn nor the dirt of their womb.
The lips that kiss the cross of Christ,
this heart which homes the spirit of God,
this flesh which shall shortly fade
will know the habit of silence, the caul of joy.
I give His priests the blood of my veins,
and prayer which flutters like songs
of meadow hummingbirds; I give my morning light,
the labor of my evening knees at work in prayer.

Though I am driven from the village by my own people
to race before wolves, bed with vipers, sleep
under the crust of snow, know painful hunger...
I shall be safe and warm and satiated
with food of the Holy Ghost, the Blessed
Sacrament of the Eucharist in communion.
I shall atone for the sins of my people,
and for my own sins of ignorance and blasphemy.
My zeal will obtain penance and my spirit peace.

Friend, be kind, accept this whip.
Like winter wind let its leather thongs
scream through the air and strike my flesh.
Like juice of the raspberry blood shall
trickle from my shoulder blades, my arms.
Each Sunday of the week I shall embrace purity.

I walk in veils and know paradise.

ROKWAHO
   1978

He dropped names on the land..
ticks sucking the earth...
De Feriet, LeRay, Herrick,
and Brown, Chaumont, Malone, Pulaski.
Out of his black robe came Kraft,
feedmills, blight, Benson Mines.
From his prayers flowed the death
of salmon and trout in mercury pools.
From letters home to his
mother settlers followed
soldiers behind hooded priests.

In his pouch he carried raisins
to cure the influenza his people
brought to the shores of the lake.
His raisins have not flourished
though his influenza remains
raging like a torrential river
flooding the banks, swallowing
fields and woods and whatever
animal standing in the way.
...
My hair and tongue are cut!

THE MAMA POEMS

"...Right-handed Twin came naturally from his mother,
the daughter, impregnated by the West Wind, of Sky-
woman. But his brother, Left-handed Twin, impatiently
sprang early from his mother's armpit and killed her
with his unnatural escape from her body."

—from the Mohawk version
of the Iroquois creation story

1911

Those fields and orchards. Barns hot with swallow flight. Your father's yellow rose bush circling the drive to the old homestead leaning into greyness, yet standing sturdy in the laughter of seven young girls ginghamed to the throat, swollen in wool though June stepped sprightly across fields and into berries brightening the meadows under larks and thrushes, pheasants fanning brush through woods of day lilies late to spring early to summer while your mama stood on the long front porch rotting beneath her feet screaming to the afternoon as her hands rose from wrinkled apron to hair whisking about her oval face shrouded in spots of anger that her seven daughters played on the neighbor's lawn.

The apple tree, translucent, yellowing the hour, ridiculous in its spiney, wobbly erection, tended with fervent hands by "Pa," arching in birth of leaf and blossom, scenting the heavy air as wisteria weights the breeze; the apple for teeth, for sauce, for Jack, for pie; the apple, symbol to your "Pa" what has been and can be in its aging bend with no new branches struggling through winter snows to break open spring. Disappointment that young Charles died a babe. The apple, shade to chickens and gobblers; the apple where your mama threw out the coffee grinds, cabbage leaves, eggshells, wet corncobs.

We loved it. Your grandma, my grandpa, you, us. (Four years ago, the house depleted in a hunter's ruin, old boards nailless from greed, old walls stripped of paper, not even a dented bedpot left in the rubble. The house down about the heads of the ghosts, crumbled into the spring cellar where brine once kept pork and pickles, where carrots and squash stayed bright and crisp. And all the voices, the voices of birth, and the wails of death, and the joy of holiday...came tumbling down.)

Oh! Mama, there was seldom happiness there. But beauty stood its ground. The earth shuddered, the fields, the orchards now bitter to the touch and the taste, the chicory, the bats of evening, the pitchers of ginger-beer, iced melon. No, there was never happiness there while your "Pa" spent his winter nights reading from the Bible in the barn, his place, allocated by your mama who would never allow his pipe in the parlor, your dirty stockings on the bedroom floor. Girls were raised to work, to carry water for the laundry, wash dishes, scrub floors, shake the tick in the morning wind, scythe the grasses, and bend, bend, forever bend in the berry fields where you bled profusely on the fruit. Your face and gingham spotted with your first knowledge, your first lesson. You were never able to wash the blood away. It stuck, hard and dark to your cheek, your hands. And you cried in the fields where iris brightened the morning still heavy with dew and night-fear, where hawks gleaned the grain of mice and woodchucks, where the mirage of old women, hideous in masks, came to pinch your arm and whisper terrible tales into your ear. Beware of the night, the shade and the wind that comes out of the west. Beware of the breath. Let me touch your hair. And it turned white. You were a child, and your hair turned white at the washer wringer. You screamed and the hideous old woman laughed a cackle that frightened the cocks crowing to the hens. And your mama spanked and took away the dessert from supper, a dish of gooseberry sauce. You wept in bed from all sorts of pain. Pain that would never leave your breasts, your breast little and as pretty as a flowerbud, a little fist that would open to mouths you never really learned to comprehend.

And the blood stayed on your cheek. It was there last month in the coffin. Brilliant in its birthmark. Not even my kiss washed it away. But the fields remain though barren without cow, a blind horse, a child's print. The fields, the land reeking with ghosts and voices gurgling the temper of the times. Depleted. Fields returning to scrub woods. And so it should be.

COMING TO AN UNDERSTANDING

You must have been a girl...
before you became my mother.

...

Remember your father's rose
bush circling the drive
where turkeys slept beneath
yellow petals in the raging sun;
remember him reading his Bible
in the barn, smoking his pipe
his wife would not allow in her parlor.
I'm sure you picked apples.

...

There is little I know.
I guess you never dreamed,
nor caught a thumb in a turtle's snap.
nor chased butterflies nor were,
in turn, chased by the bull
snorting in childhood meadows.

...

How can I continue without
knowing, without stopping
the blood from your cut finger,
licking your batter bowl, choking.

SOMETIMES, INJUSTICE

The day I was born my father bought me a .22.
A year later my mother traded it for a violin.
Ten years later my big sister traded that
for a guitar, and gave it to her boyfriend...
who sold it.

Now you know why I never learned to hunt,
or learned how to play a musical instrument,
or became a Wall Street broker.

Mama Failed to Kill the Rat...

Mama failed to kill the rat
when it ran across my bed
that November my father tore the wall away
building the new addition to the house.
Snow seeped in, and not only snow:
raccoon thought it a good winter place;
squirrel cached hickory nuts.
Mama stood in the doorway
with a lamp in her grip
and told me not to move.

Since then rodents, mice have
always meant change to me, dead
or alive; a different course.

When corn leans, chestnuts fall;
when neighbors take in the screens
and fishermen put away
hooks and poles, late autumn,
I don't sleep so very well,
but still see Mama in the doorway
in the light of that kerosene flame
her face contorted in the mask
of chilled horror.

Mice have always meant change to me.
I hear rats gnawing the floor.

INHERITANCE

Your pleasure was running.
to be on the go, downtown
to try on hats where you got lice once
and brought them home to us.
When you learned to drive
his Chevy you drove us to Canada.
They wouldn't let you cross the bridge
President Roosevelt built for us
because you weren't a citizen
of these United States.

Your running taught me how to run.
I keep Greyhound rich.
However, I learned
from your embarrassment never
to try on hats or cross bridges
into lands where I am not wanted.

WAKE

In coffin light
I played with cobwebs...
hammock strung from corner
to corner knowing she slept
the winter day and winter cold
through the baked salmon supper,
whiskey drunk behind the barn
the arrival of old aunts
and young cousins

I remember the white of her hair
bunned and hidden behind
the waxened face shorn of breath;
they had her clench a blue rosary
which brought meadows to her cheeks
and swallows to her lips
sealed then and finally with paraffin

Women climbed the stairs
with sleeping children in their arms,
others carried bowls of succotash
to tables crowded with hunger
as men sang songs;
I touched her stiffness with my lips:
there was music in her hands
and I would hear their stories

PICKING BLACKBERRIES

Monday sun slants across the bush,
August brushes your hair in wind
off Lake Ontario; the watch
ticks at your wrist while the kids
squabble over who has the larger can,
the most berries, the blackest tongue.

Mrs. Anthony telling
stories in your ear
over berries meant for pie
to please your man
who might come tonight...
"The way to a man's heart
is through his belly."
You know that is a lie.

Your qualities were never baking,
but when you rolled up the sleeves
and baited your own hook,
or cleaned a mess of trout
or string of November rabbits
even when we demanded you darn
socks or heal blisters, fight
a cold...you spent years pleasing
what was not to be pleased,
darning where there were no holes,
picking berries more to gossip
with Mrs. Anthony than for pies,
forgetting teeth
needed tending, taking up
a glass of water in the dark
when Mary cried in fever,
or sitting at the winter window

watching snow in tears
telling us when he will come,
when he will go with no
understanding of what love is.

There's a plastic plant on his grave.
Yours is marked, name
chiseled into stone, the fence
around erected, prayer cards
about ready to be printed,
and still you have no idea
of what picking blackberries
was all about, you would bend
an ear to Mrs. Anthony
telling stories...
"The way to a man's heart
is through his stomach."

The end of the week, rain every day;
the lake is black in storm, Agnes' kids
are just about all married. You placed
the old watch in the dresser drawer,
and write letters to the family saying
how sorry you are to have missed sending
Christmas presents this year, and that
Mary's arthritis is getting worse.

...

Sparrows and wrens pick the blackberries.

Joshua Clark
Three Mile Bay, N.Y.
July 1979

*"Kind and loving husband
and tender to your flock."*
—gravestone epitaph

I
name stained in colored glass
on the Baptist window erected
in the English spirit of your fervor

let me tell you, Pastor Joshua,
great-great-great grandfather,
bred in the clover spring of 1802,
bed to Sybil, sire of Mary,
sire to the stones of this
seedy cemetery bloody from veins
opened to the summer breeze,
let me tell you, Joshua,
even your bones are dust.
the headstone chips in the sun
white asters climb
moisture of the grasses
wending across your name

yes, let me tell you, Joshua Clark,
your great-grandson married
the Seneca girl whose father's land
you stole, and his brother drunk
in the velvet parlor lifted cup
by cup the earth to the tavern keeper's smile
yes, my grandfather paid it away, too,
acre by acre to maids who came to dust

his wife's music room and to hired hands
who plowed his father's fields
until only your church and cemetery plot
were left and safe from their foolishness
Joshua, the apple trees have claimed
the house, sumac fill the cellar bins,
the stone foundations bed mice,
and snakes prowl your yellow roses
where once you sat in the shade, counting souls
drinking ginger-beer
eyeing the westerly sun
black with barn swallows.
your woods are cleared, hickory axed;
there is not a single creek
in those meadows, even bats
and hawks have fled;
your blood has thinned into a trickle...
I claim very little and pass nothing on...
not a drop to any vein.

your siring is finished, deeds done
and, accomplishments or not, only a name
remains penned into an old family Bible
and stained in glass, purple and green,
of a church no one visits
but skunks and black spiders;
there are enough babies squawking anyway.

II

you were a strong man, strong as the elms
which once reared over the front lawn
and the white pine which fenced the fruit
orchard where ginghamed Sybil plucked
sweet cherry and damson plum

and teased your loins with her pretty English face
her thin ankle and narrow waist;
you were a strong man in the blood
your sap ran April
and you fathered our centuries, our wars
our treacheries, our lies,
our disappointing lives, loves; your fingers
coiled the rope which bound and trussed us all
on the hanging tree, the roots of our feet
dangling over the earth wet with blood
rockets exploding about our ears
deaf and blind as your drunken grandson
to the waste of blackberry brambles
and the loud gnawing of rats in the sweat
of your goose down mattress where Sybil birthed
Mary and all the dawns of your hairy thighs

old cats purr on the supper table
of cold beef; goats munch clean
meadows in the twilight of
birch bending to the rainbows of mornings past.

III

Patty-Lyn and Craig
never read your epitaph,
nor knelt in your Baptist church nor tasted
Sybil's plum preserves, nor haven't
the slightest thought that Ely Parker
was a great Seneca General who had little to do
with your Baptist God.
hands were unfinned, unwebbed for tools
to preserve and beget and protect
all that's beautiful in trout and mallard
all which is remarkable in fire and ice

all which is noble in blood and loin
all which births and dies
in the raging sunset, of dawn;
this half-blood Mohawk condemns your church
to ash and though I would not tamper with the earth
which holds your dust I would chip the stone
flake by flake that heralds your name and deeds
but carry pails of fresh water to the green cedar
rooting in your family plot where my bones
refuse to lay coiled and pithed in the womb
of a tribe which has neither nation nor reason nor drum

my father claims my blood
and sired in the shadow of a turtle my growls
echo in the mountain woods where a bear climbs down
rocks to walk across your grave to leave its prints
upon the summer dust and pauses to sniff a wild hyssop
and break open a beehive for the honey of the years
and smack its lips on red currants

old cats should be wild and feed on field mice.
Joshua, I've nearly lost the essence of your name
and cannot hear the murmur of your time.
I stand throwing rocks at the stained glass
of your fervor knowing time ceases with the crash,
the tinkle of the stones striking glass,
and all our blood between the installation
and the retribution has vaporized into the bite
of a single mosquito sucking my arm
in the summer breeze of this seedy cemetery

now sleep

BLACK RIVER, SUMMER 1981

For Patti-Lynn

The evening river carries no sound...
not the bark of this fox whose skull
weights my hand,
nor the wind of this hawk
feather tucked into the buttonhole of my shirt.

Rivers grumble and hiss and gurgle;
they roar and sing lullabies;
rivers rage and flow and dance
like unseen wind;
in the dark they carry the eyes
of stars and footprints of deer.

      I have slept on your arm
      dawn sweetening my mouth,
      stiff in limb
      and rose to your morning song.

      I have watched geese fly over,
      eels slither downstream,
      bullheads defy rapids,
      spiders ripple waves
      in trapped inlets along the shore,
      fireflies light paths
      from murky banks
      to mysterious islands
      where witches live.

      I have studied your waters:

      Daydreamed my watch to listen,

to feel your tremble,
to learn your summer,
touch your winter,
and be content.

TELEPHONE CALL

He's going to Alaska
to pick tulips this time.

You're there?
I've been dialing wrong numbers.

I fell the other day.
Hurt my back. My liver pains.

No, I eat, I say I eat.
He cooked a TV dinner
and told me I was strong enough
to wash the supper dishes.
My bones ache.

This time he's going to pick tulips.
Where? Well, maybe it is
the lilac festival in Rochester.
I don't know why he wants to go to Alaska.
Said I fell on purpose so he couldn't go.
I don't care where he goes.

Mary works hard making pies and boiling stews
for those priests. Her cat is dead. Killed
on the highway, Found it in a heap of blood
in the snow. She's lonely. They gave her a dog.
It won't stay home either.

Jennie's thin. Mere bones,
but she stays on the road selling Avon.

No, I never hear from Agnes.
She's one daughter I've lost, I guess.

Oh! yes. My nurse comes,
but hasn't been here for two weeks.
I cleaned all my house before
the cleaning woman came. Couldn't
have her find it dirty.

Why does he want to go to Alaska to pick tulips?
Well, good night, Write.

May, 1980

MAMA

For Helene
On Her 30th Birthday

The runt of the litter
of seven little girls.

I don't want to spend
too much time on the idea
of how deprived you were.
There is already too much
pity in this world,
nor get saccharine about you
rocking me to sleep in your arms
and baking bread in a hot oven,
or breaking your back
in a field of blueberries.
Nor remind you of how you favored
my sister, or denied me for the man
whose puke you've cleaned up for years.
I've pretty much forgotten that.
However, I doubt we ever forgive.
There's enough distance now
to separate fact from fiction
and to remind myself
you were/are a woman...
capable of being human...
your skin wrinkles as does mine,
your flesh withers.
We're of the same cut;
the same cotton cloth.
I knew your wet nipples;
you knew my sharp teething.

Mama, they called
very late the other night.
Woke me up at 3 a.m.
What could I say at such an hour,
what could I do.
I couldn't rock you in my arms,
nor stuff you into a tote bag
and ride Greyhound to California
where you'd be safe in the sun.
Nor could I convince them
that a woman is not a Ford,
that when it stops running
you take it to the junkyard
and sell it for used parts.
They wouldn't buy that.

      Mama, we're all runts.

Eventually we'll all
be placed away from ourselves
where we can't harm
ourselves; where the tough
and strong won't need to worry
nor interrupt the baseball game
to check if we're all right
lighting the kitchen stove.

Mama, shake your head.
Bite the first hand that puts
a finger on your arm.
The moon is rising on the woods.
The apples ripen.
Some crazy hound howls down the road.
The neighbors watch *All
in the Family*

while the kid stands in the dark
of the stairwell crying
for a glass of Coke.
Cops crawl through the night
looking for trouble to start.
Joe St. Louis is drunk again.
One day he'll freeze in the snow
on the way home from the bar.

Mama, shake your head.
It's up to you to fight.
That place is full to the rafters
with folks that wouldn't bite,
I know, Mama, I was there...
remember.

DECEMBER

Set up the drum.
Winter's on the creek.

Dark men sit in dark kitchens.
Words move in the air.
A neighbor is sick.
Needs prayer.

Women thaw frozen
strawberries.

In the dark...a drum.

> Kids hang out
> eating burgers
> at McDonald's.
> The Williams boy
> is drunk

Set up the drum.

Berries thaw,
are crushed,
fingers stained, and tongues.

Set up the drum
A neighbor is sick.
Say a prayer.
Dark men sit in dark kitchens.

Wind rattles the moon.

MAY 15, 1982
Three Mile Bay, New York

I've failed often; this was my worst failure.

They took the red casket from the winter vault
while I was riding Greyhound in California.
No excuse.

It was a lovely day Aunt Ruth wrote.
Spring and lilac. Dandelions. Blue sky, a few clouds,
a fishing boat in the bay. Perfect.
                                    Not many there:
Mary, Ruth and Jennie, and Martin hobbling on his
new cane. Mary said he ordered a nice headstone,
and showed stress signs of his loneliness, regret,
shame for the abuse of years. Too late. I don't know
if a preacher was there. It wouldn't revive you,
nor ease pain you knew in your depths.

I used to believe in the powers of death.
Until you died.
It was the last belief.
I believe in echoes now,
in earth that holds you. I believe in a bird,
its flight, though I'm not sure which one, hawk
or seagull; the cedar near your grave, and the lake
not far away that you feared from childhood.
Summer is here on the chicory, harvest is next,
then winter which chilled, always, your arms.
I believe in seasons, time, too, I'd suppose.
There isn't much between mewl and rattle...
an occasional laugh at some human joke,
and more hurt than the human heart can bear;
disappointment, and the terrible lack of love.

I won't tally the balance sheet.

I miss you.

I'm sorry I failed. This time I can't say
I won't do it again, because I probably would.

You might be happy now. You're where you wanted to be...
in the Bay under the cedar near your father,
who you loved. He was a good man you always said.
Perhaps the only man who was kind.

I'm saccharine.
I don't mean to be. Dying isn't a ruined dinner.
I mean to be truthful, sincere, dispassionate...
which is difficult...forthright. I mean
to remember you as I ride the Greyhound in the dark,
or pick berries or stroke my cat, or burn rice.
I'm not good at elegies...not even yours, my mother,
condolences, buying plants, telephoning, saying
thank you...as I wasn't good at kissing cheeks, or
showing up for supper on time. But you lied
for me then...as you lied for all your men.
Perhaps you'll lie again for me now that I fail.

REVERBERATION

A north wind heard is heard always.
Drums reverberate like circles on a disturbed pool
into an incomprehensible time;
the banging of the drum does not stop
once thumped in the ceremony of life.

How can I explain optical illusion?
Can I cut her heart muscle into tiny pieces,
her brain, and set these pieces down on paper,
or in the palm of my hand? Memory weeds chaff.
Attempting to re-create the woman she was
through jottings of conversation, hand movements,
facial expressions, thought pattern, she
becomes a quirk of the imagination.
There remains a strong need in the blood,
strong in the verb orphaned in loneness,
roots pulled out by the hair. Are lips
still too close to nipple and breath.
Will she also come and sit at midnight.

I'll chatter with shadows filtering rooms,
watch the rocking chair rock, smell an apple pie
bubbling in a cold oven, hear a teacup smash
on the floor of a vacant kitchen, or hear whispers
in the parlor where there are no voices.

They stay where they are wanted...

1982

Home. To fields and woods. To the frightening river I shied and the hills my horse cropped early June mornings. The fence that tore my calf when Lightning panicked and took me over the fence and cliff. The scar remains indelibly creased on the flesh. It is for this reason I remember, and I remember nearly everything.

I etch on the walls of my study. Hawk's feathers, a swallow's nest, sweetgrass, pebbles, and old boards that collect dust each time the imaginary tick sucks blood from behind my ear. I carry out yellowed snapshots. Grandpa leading his white horse to the trough. You big with Mary Agnes in your arms...myself not the twinkle of your wildest thought, or fear. You loved photographs. Your walls crawled with them...Martin, in war uniform proudly riding a tank; Pat in his Marine blues; Mary, young and beautiful, her eyes flashing. Agnes dressed in her Catholic uniform from the Conservatory. Myself, a snip of adolescent confidence. A known lie. Façade. They all wore façades. And you believed in them. It was all you had to believe. Photos that left old dust marks on the walls when he took them down and threw your dreams in the garbage. You sat night after night with the album by your side on the couch, usually with your arthritic hand touching your babies, what you thought were your loved ones. (Do you know my father secretly carried your snap in his pocket until he died?) Is life merely a photograph? For some. For you.

He let you die alone. He told no one. Deprived. Depleted like your old homestead. The hunter took the kill and left you a crumble of old bones like boards, broken windowpanes. You went into death without a yellow rose from your father's circle. Denied. Your spirit as thin and transparent as Saran. You hated cold. And you were freezing. February. And all your hopes lay in tubes and vials. I can see you spitting up your hospital supper. I can hear you say, *I must lose weight,* though you weighed barely eighty pounds. Eighty pounds of disappointment and hurt. He allowed you to die alone. The man you feigned adoration for, the man whose puke soiled your age, whose vomit of cheap sweet wine you bent and cleaned. OH! Mama, he didn't love you. He didn't even like your cooking. You became a drag on his cane. You were his cane and his hammer and his claw. You became everything despicable to him. Until now. Now that you are a part of the root of that cedar on your father's grave next to you. Now he remembers how beautiful your face had been and how straight your back, and firm your breast, how sweet your mouth. Now he touches reality. His right foot is about to step into shadow. You are revenged. Not that you probably want to be. But I want you to be revenged...for everything. Even my own father, who was as cruel as his love could be, as any love, as all love can be. Even though he carried your snapshot into the rattle of his death.

We're still reaching for an understanding. Of so many things.

You stayed a girl. Withered age was merely a mask. Your flirt was always on the fingertip as it pressed a hand, or placed a wedge of pie before a guest. You lived crossing the bridge into Canada. You never really learned you can't cross into lands where you aren't wanted. (Nor have I, really.) You never got the lice completely out of your hair. You couldn't cut cords of any kind. You never buried the placentas. Like a boy you played mumblety-peg and lost each time you played. What was your final happiness? Your father's grave. To know Ruth and Jennie were there watching the men shovel the earth. Your sisters admitted to loving you.

IS SUMMER THIS BEAR

OSHERANOHA
        (Wolverine)

Under breeze
in the light
of the new moon
of the wild strawberry
into the roots
and shadows
of this clump of sumac
I give you
this old tooth
so you
will return it
straight and strong.

tekiatatenawiron

12 Moons

Midnight. Winds tossed my wisdom-
tooth to wolverine and darkness,
sumac. It was not returned as promised,
strong and sharp.
      Again I go
with my myths to fisher. Perhaps
the moon this time in scent of river
water and wild raspberry will
be truthful. Or I shall smoke
in leaves gone dry in summer.

—Akwesasne
Summer, 1984

WOLF

prints in snow
scat on paths
hairs clinging to low bushes
howl on the moon

    i pull up blankets
    put the book down
    turn out the light
    and sleep again
    with your breath on my cheek

mountains move in your trot
in your smell
survive in your young
grow in the strength of your wisdom:
turtle and bear
welcome you home

REDTAIL

Eye to eye we meet
     in my city smell
disbelief in blood
     flecked in your pupil
     my chin razor-chipped
caged in the mountains
     you would take pecks of skin
     I would collect tail feathers
     you would fall to earth
     I would rise on wind
I doubt we would survive

I stared at you with wonder
     wing eyed for years:
wheeling, perched, crunching bones
     on flat river-rock
You've ignored my presence
     now you must face me
deciding the poisons in my blood
deciding my heart

I have no advantage even though you are caged
     wire separated your claw
     from my liver, finger
capable of pulling the trigger

I am struck, vanquished, knowledgeable
You are too few and I too many
     you are shrew, woodchuck
     I am weed and weasel
     while you soar I thief

Eye to eye we meet
      in your meadow
      I am bee and buttercup
      fumed in strange smell
You are mole and berry seed
      you guard the east and home
      you clean the sky of vermin
      you lick the bloody stone
Where I have opened veins
      and split the bark
      wearing otter skin

LISTENING FOR THE ELDERS

is summer this bear
        home this tamarack
are these wild berries song
is this hill
        where my grandmother sleeps
        this river where
        my father fishes

does this winter-house
        light its window for me
        burn oak for my chill
does this woman sing my pain
does this drum beat
        sounding waters
or does this crow caw
does this hickory nut fall
        this corn ripen
        this field yellow
        this prayer-feather hang
        this mother worry
        this ghost walk
does this fire glow
        this bat swoop
        this night fall
does this star shine
        over mountains
        for this cousin who has
        no aunt picking sweetgrass
        for a pillow

is summer this wolf
        this elm leaf
        this pipe smoke

is summer this turtle
       home this sumac
       home this black-ash
is summer this story
is summer home
is twilight home
is summer this tongue
       home this cedar
       these snakes in my hair

reflection on this sky
       this summer day
       this bear

GRAVEYARDS

My friend looked a little jittery.
I told Dennis that yes I could handle
the situation alone. Just get in your car
and slowly mosey on down the road...
no need for you to get busted.

There were the men...stones sitting in a row.
Little Belly, Young King, Tall Peter,
Deerfoot, Captain Pollard, Destroy Town,
Red Jacket and General Ely S. Parker.

To see their headstones under October sun
in that cemetery I remembered how Ford
and Helen took me for a drive the day before
through the mountains along the highway which
aproned the Kinzua dam to find Cornplanter's grave.
The black cat which crossed our lost
country way misled us into several wild-
goose chases. So we headed back toward
Salamanca where I was to read poems in the new
library. Funny. We laughed pretty hard afterwards,
Helen and Robert and Ford, because we sat
in that sterling new library waiting for an audience
which hadn't been invited. One young woman,
a student, I guess, came to our table
in the children's section and expressed how much
she loved poetry and how much she would love to stay
and hear poems, but well, next time I came to
Salamanca, not then. Tomorrow was
a school day and she had phys-ed homework.
The four of us balled up in the yellow jalopy,
drove off to find Jerry Rothenberg's old house
in town and a Dunkin' Donuts figurin' the town

didn't want any hostile Mohawk reading poems
to their Seneca Indians. I cashed the fat check
when I got back to Buffalo...real fast with thanks.

Anyway, as I said, I told Dennis to get in the car,
start the motor, and leave slow. I was gonna cause
trouble. I'm really pretty proud of him, a white guy.
He did turn the ignition on, did start the motor,
but waited for my messy trouble to commence.

Right in the heart of Little Belly's stomach
stood an American flag in the traditional
"red, white and blue"...not synonymous
with "turtle, bear and wolf." The flag lifted
from the earth easily, and its stick broke neatly in half.

Dennis had the ol' car revved up and the door opened.
I threw down the stick and climbed aboard.

Which reminds me. Do you know the U.S. Post Office
recently printed a thirteen-cent stamp to commemorate
Crazy Horse, the Lakota warrior? The proclamation
said because Crazy Horse had been,
and I quote, "a Great American." I think
the government is searching out his hidden grave now
to plant a small flagpole on it, too.

KAHERAWAK'S BIRTHDAY—JULY 28

My First Granddaughter

Crow caws against grey skies,
flies nibble the elbow as a breeze
off the summer river lifts hair
from my face waiting for sun after rain.
Letters to friends are waiting, sealed,
for posting as black-eyed susans and goldenrod
sway in down-fields bursting blooms
as dried raspberry pellets thump earth
from brambles that have completed
the labor of centuries. Noon slowly
approaches with the whistle of a train
riding the rails across the river in Canada,
disturbs the tabby cat's sleep under another
screech of crow flapping wings high
over the island. Movement by stealth, like spider,
sun at last emerges in the southern sphere.
Things splash yellow...even green leaves
of sumac and poplar are tainted, brushed.
Finch sings a warning to starling,
swallow zooms through the air expecting insects;
the currant is bare, the berries eaten by goats;
corn is dry but beans are heavy and onions
ready for pulling.

      This is your birthday gift...
this summer day and all its riches; snores
of the dog, heal-all, purple burdock,
thistle; winds and birds, weasel in the grass,
mice in the barn, berries jammed for winter, spiders,
grandma's smile, sun, turtle slipping from mud,
bear reaching into gnarled trees for honey, wolf
roaming the distant Adirondacks

and Grandmother Moon waning now in late July,
commanding her strength

to rise again tonight to bathe the dark
in colors of harvest orange which will tip
bat wings, stars and clouds drifting,
and move the river to the sea,
illuminate western wind, bring good dreams
to your sleep, happy days to your
accumulating years on this earth, years
in which you will learn to thank the sun,
Grandmother Moon, the corn and beans and squash,
the berries, herbs, the useful birds and dragonflies,
bees, the elm and maple that reach at night
to stars that guide the hunter in the woods, light
the fisherman's path and glisten
on the scales of the fish themselves.
You will learn to thank the mysteries,
movements above and below the earth,
below the four winds, the four colors,
the four directions.
       Tonight
your father will play his guitar and sing a song
and then have a good, long smoke
while crow sleeps in its nest away from your dreams
under the lingering scent of strawberry leaves.

This is your birthday gift...
the old stories of the sky, waters, the earth
and winds. One day when old you, too,
will tell them on into time within the sounds
of the drum, the quiet of the mountain,
the silent flow of the river. Yes, good dreams,
good journey, many moons,
and sweet winds for your pillow.

Cornwall Island, Akwesasne 1983

GREYHOUNDING THIS AMERICA

A Partial Explanation

Thoughts of John Berryman

All month the moon has been reaching
for the pear tree. Now the black fruit
and leaves move in wind off the marsh.
A fox yips across the wide meadow;
raspberries and the sea scent the air.

Conversation is slow, stilted...
words hard as the August pears, color
of the leaves...though the moon
threads its light over quiet faces.
The house dog groans in the dark

neither scenting basil in the dooryard
nor aware of the fox's pain under the stars;
the moon moves through the sour apple
and drops among juniper and oak.
"Ciao!" The apt response..."Ciao."

FOR CHEROKEE MARIE
Who May Have Forgotten

earth strong in the blood
fleas cannot suck from veins
blood rich in the sun

mountains explode on the chest
of western plains, birds scale
clouds over broken graves

torn by wolves and puppies
blood feeds berries, the white bones
of Crazy Horse were never found

the lance flowers the earth
blood thickens as braided hair
the spider spins in the sun

SAND CREEK, COLORADO
100 Years After

Night thick as heavy voices
or the plod of cattle rattling
in the farmer's garbage dump

coyotes called ancient shadows
Cheyenne whose fires burn low along the creek
to light the collection of the dead
bones wolves chose not to chew

the state marker says nothing
of the women, the children
or White Antelope's cry...
"nothing lasts but grass and mountains..."
choked by the butt of his penis
soldiers thought a joke

wandering in sacred screams
holy terror and extermination
picking the snot of gold from Chivington's nose
he stuffed to the stench of his kill

thin hands found our faces
our dog whined and hid beneath the Datsun
hungry mouths of children
sought her breasts and would have sucked
had she opened her blouse

sleep was safe in New York
exhausted in the numb and nulled morning
we counted cigarette packages, beer cans
orange peels and civilization
and left the dead to comfort the dying

while in the dark birds sing

history's blood has grown its spring crop of grass
tall cottonwoods stand central to the scholar
lofty rock peak dawn to citron morning

THE YELLOWSTONE

I.
The cat paws of dawn scratch
the edges of the Yellowstone
while overhead the sky fills with brightness
and under orange cottonwoods startle
the eastern eye, worry the deer.
The morning whistles flushed out rabbits
and three pheasants frightened into flight.
The Yellowstone has been turning since creation,
and dawn has been falling down mountains
to drift into coulees before the first arrow was shaped.

II.
The conductor punched tickets in Butte, Montana;
gold trickled out of the Rockies, out of Shoshone blood!

III.
This river knows no other course...
nor does the Ohio nor the Missouri;
the Yellowstone has shared its waters and beavers
with all explorers, slaked the Crow's thirst
and Red Cloud and even Custer.

The river moves on.
The train doesn't lose sight of the shoreline
and the mallards and geese and stark willows
and the antelope paths leading into canyons;
and ghosts fishing its pools
and the dark and sacred mountains rising.

The explorer stops to hunt,
the hunter to war,
the warrior to occupy,

the occupier to ranch.
This river moves on.
Geese fly north to Canada.

IV.
When the summer sun is hottest the river
will shrivel...wait for winter snow;
it will narrow under wild plum trees;
it will fatten with the inevitable April floods.
The river moves on
slowly across the land, stark and dusty,
red with the blood of Crazy Horse,
silent to the echoes of shrapnel and the thud
of falling flesh; the waters move
though raccoons come to drink
and trout hide in secluded pools.

V.
James Welch drinks a beer
in Missoula,
and writes his poems.

VI.
The Yellowstone creates no music, no noise...
even the rapids' whisper is deadened
by the glass pane of the passing window;
it feeds the locoweed and the magpie
and the children of Sacajawea.
It collects no taxes and builds no temples.
It takes nothing along with it
but perhaps a fallen chinaberry or Hereford
or the broken wing feather of an eagle.
This river moves on.
it pushes a little mud,
leaves a little silt,

sucks a little sun.
The Yellowstone changes its course slowly,
it forgets the empire,
it leaves an islet in the stream;
uncovers rock, bones of old ones;
possibly a rusty musket of Colter or Bridger,
or the bleached jaw of an elk
caught in the bite of a winter blizzard.

VII.
Buffalo thundered the shores,
children bathed in its waters,
Black Elk prayed to its spirit.

VIII.
The Yellowstone contracts and purples to dusk;
evening stars rumple upon an eddy;
the moon rises over ripples;
mosquitoes spurt from the shoreline;
raven roost cottonwoods;
an owl whispers; coyote sniffs mice.

The train moves into Idaho at night
through the mountain country of Montana,
the home of the Crow and Cheyenne,
We drift into a conclave of stars.
The river moves on
under the smoke of the train within
the time of an eye, and a drum; within
the time of a rifle and plow
and the hoof of sheep rutting the grasses
with teeth which have nibbled the hills bare.

IX.
Ghosts wail by campfires
under those Yellowstone stars.
Black Elk prayed.
A rabbit fears its skin, its flesh
as the hunter steps through the brush.
A goose honks in the darkness.
The Yellowstone follows its course.
Deer come to drink!
The train whistle blows in the night
over the flow of the river.
I close my notebook for sleep,
remembering that Reno was probably drunk
and Custer ambitious.

X.
In the morning a hawk will take the skies!

MONET

Tsalie, Arizona

blue sage purple
within the red desert

caught in the crow's shadow
seeking higher clouds

where your brush and my pen
may not scale these colors

light drips off fingertips
into pools of image

sage, pinion-blue, blue
against blue, and time tips

petals; heat waves
rise from this bunch of sage

blue in the dawn
scarlet in the sun.

light peels like bark
on junipers, my hands remain empty.

WHEN IN REALITY

I wrote in my journal
I had eaten only an orange
and some cheese this morning,
and drunk a pot of coffee dry.
When in truth, at dawn, I had eaten
lizards, coyotes, silver and cactus
and a lone laborer in the desert.
I drank sky, sun and clouds;
my eyes consumed plains, mountains,
countries, continents;
worlds rumbled in my belly.
Tonight I slice and fork the western moon,
crunch on stars
and drink the whine of wolves.

CANYON DE CHELLY, RETURN, 1978

For Jim Ruppert

I.
From the rim, noon and the crow
are the very same. Imagination
cannot break those ancient ruins.

II.
Enter from Chinle, the floor absorbs;
knowledge clatters like cottonwood leaves
turning August gold; moon sketched on walls
where turkeys run. We have not perceived
the rhythm of the drum, nor our eyes
identified the dancers' steps, nor worn
antelope skins about the loins.

III.
Marauding Spaniards, or Kit Carson's
thieving recruits...we enter seeking
ripe peaches and the touch of crumbled walls.

Three crows fly darkening skies;
Willie Mustache tells old stories,
old horrors of search and destroy,
that Anasazi youths once scaled
those unscaleable cliffs before Coca
Cola invented rheumatism.

IV.
Our presence has shifted light;
cigarette stubs, the lead gasoline fumes
are hammers against adobe dust.
We have gawked at the flesh,
and contorted, tattooed shadows.

V.
Exit. Supper in Chinle:
hamburgers, iced tea. We have moved
with clouds, the blue bunting
which followed our truck, but have not
left a peach stone to gather time.
We go home to watch movies on tv
and calculate diplomas and salaries.

VI
Lookouts on the rim designate
the past, lean into time. From the rim
we can revere both the star and the crow,
and those people who defied destiny
by clinging to walls with tooth and nail,
absorbed in the task of surviving brutal winds.

NOVEMBER SIERRAS, 1976

For Peter

Moon partially eaten
by hungry coyotes
yapping on the hills for mice.
Sugar pine cones drop in the dark
of the raccoon forest;
firefly stars hang in manzanita brush;
two men on stumps huddled
over mugs of steaming cedar tea;
huddled over words on frosty air;
shivering, we heard coyote sing,
and talked of home north
in the Adirondacks
sitting on the ridge
in that brittle light.
The moon shifted tall ponderosas.

Mohawks in Paiute country;
and speechless Louis arguing
with phantoms of the November sleep!
Rosebud tracking moles!

Our words touched
as the mugs
and our poems!
We pissed and entered
the cabin...you to Sarah,
and my hypered exhaustion
to the moonlit bunk
near the wood stove.

There is no message, Peter,
but the yapping of the dogs
and the falling of the moon
and the freeze on the dawn.

WANDA ON THE SEASHORE
Pacifica

You gleam the sea, you and your beachcomber
With the fiery beard and the glinting eye;
You are the sea, you and your friend,
Dunking-in-the-raw of the red light of the sun
On into the smile of the moon, taking a beer, coffee;
Cooking the fish you caught;
Gathering shells...the weird wind in your hair...;
Clamming with your big toes in the sand and mud;
Hunting ghost crabs, scraping mussels;
Your hut...broken, airy...leans as the wind leans
Through domes of dunes above the shore in range
Of storms. You have a hell of a time,
You and your beachcomber and the mongrel dog;
You steal off and find a field of painted-Indian-brush
Somewhere along the road, your skirt swollen
Falling around your legs and thighs,
Your fingers stained from wild blackberries.
You are living the sea, dining on grass,
Fingering the dark greenness of the woods.
I am grey in this great grey city!

READING POEMS IN PUBLIC

I stand on a stage and read poems,
poems of boys broken on the road;
the audience tosses questions.

I tell of old chiefs swindled of their daughters,
young braves robbed of painted shields,
Medicine Man hitting the bottle;
I chant old songs in their language
of the Spirit in wind and water...
they ask if Indians shave.

I recite old stories,
calendar epics of victory battles,
and cavalry dawn massacres on wintered plains,
villages where war ponies are tethered to snow...
and they want to know
how many Indians commit suicide.

I read into the microphone,
I read into the camera,
I read into the printed page,
I read into the ear...
and they say what a pretty ring you wear.
The tape winds, the camera reels,
the newspaper spins
and the headlines read:
Ruffian, the race horse, dies in surgery.

At the end of the reading they thank me;
go for hamburgers at McDonalds
and pick up a six-pack to suck as they watch the death
of Geronimo on the late show.

I stand on a stage and read poems,
and read poems, and read...

HUMORS AND/OR NOT SO HUMOROUS

On Second Thought

I never wanted to live in Brooklyn
with the ghosts of Crane, Wolfe and Mailer.
I never wanted to live in Brooklyn
after all your pleadings.
I hate crossing bridges
and wondering if I've crossed the right one;
or if I looked back I'd find
it consumed by the river.

I moved to Brooklyn
when you moved to Chicago;
and I've been enjoying the view
and the walk across the bridge
even if I can't spot Redhook
or hit a boat below with spit,
or catch a star.
I've never wanted to live in Brooklyn,
but I've been enjoying the ghosts
of Crane, Wolfe and Mailer.

HEARD POEM
Studio Museum Book Fair

"I used
to have
a Cherokee
boyfriend.
I knew
he was
Indian
because
he could see
a road sign
three miles
away."

THE COMET

Seattle, Washington

In the bar
a Mohawk sings, a drum
beats song into beer
bottles, coffee mugs, ears.
Coins tinkle into a hat.
While
in the men's room
atop the urinal
standing before erotic
scribbles and slogans
over the rain of piss
a vase of iris and spring
pussy willows
embarrasses the pisser
with surprise and joy.

Macho
holding himself
with poems drumming
in the bowl
cannot compromise
with beauty.

Song enters
iris tickles spine as he turns
zips up for the next beer; rain
outside hides Mt. Rainer
but feeds sky and earth.

Confused by beauty
in such odd places
he drops his coin
amongst the tinkles in the hat.

YOUNG MALE

You sat quietly across the subway aisle...
raucous thunder howling in your throat,
thunder which would gag the breeze in mine.
Your tight fists are caked with sludge of cement;
hands which would slaughter six million buffalo
on the range if there were six million buffalo.
Instead, you build nuclear reactors.

Your hair is soft and loose, sports a blonde sheen;
hazel eyes send out suspicious messages,
afraid I'll scalp those flowing locks
tearing the bloody membrane from your head.
You squat on the subway seat like a mountainman
of the old as-yet-unconquered West, a green blade
ready to skin beaver or any cuss you don't much like
the crook of his jaw. Your thighs bulge, your heavy arms
are thick with electrical power of whips.
I wonder if there is a smile in your soul.
Can you bend to sniff a violet?
I doubt you'd scent anything but a double
whiskey, a hooker on the curb, your hunting boots,
your own rawness.
                    Your face is not ugly
nor does it appear particularly mean, even
those hazel eyes don't seem too cruel, but when I look
at those hands knotted in a crisp clench
I know you would crush me on a whim
for you are America...
not the land, rivers, mountains, desert or sky,
not hawk or wolf. You are the superhighways,
skyscrapers, acid streams clogged with dead rainbows and
you are Gary, Indiana; downtown L.A., Burger King,
"adult bookstores," Ronald Reagan, New Jersey

that stole the Giants and now teases the American Exchange.
Your prowess rumbles as the subway slides through
the harbor tunnel to Bowling Green Station;
when the doors open, you stand. I'm amazed to see
how short you are, shorter than me by an inch or two,
but bulky in rump and flank. We ascend the escalator;
you tramp off towards Broad Street; I amble to the Post
Office in the old Cunard Building to send letters home.
I know you are here to stay
and that you are scouting buffalo.

SOFKY
SEMINOLE SOUP

it takes lye,
more lye
to make it
have good taste...
sweet...
with salt and black pepper

and boil
boil
boil

(Charley told me
in Oklahoma City)

FRIENDSHIP DAYS AT AKWESASNE
Summer of '84...Annual Event

For Francis

Humid afternoon by the St. Lawrence,
women canoe-racers paddle the river;
full of fry-bread, soda and hot
strawberry-rhubarb pie.
I stumble under the cedar arbor
to listen to the drum and singing.

Outfitted Mohawks circle a "stomp dance."
I take a place on a bench near
an elder woman who asks in Mohawk,
"What do you do?" Tote bag slung over my
left shoulder I figure I should own up.
"I'm a writer,"...in smiles.
"What kind?" she asks, really curious.
"A poet," I reply proudly...
to which she offers a grunt,
gets up from the bench and huffs off.

Well, maybe she's right.

OJIBWA

Cornwell Island, Ontario

river steeped in moving storm
clouds and lightning reflected
on the sheen
          he sat on the hillock
sketching; chicory, black-
eyed susans guarded the flesh
of his naked back etched by hay,
stamped, tattooed with a scarlet rose

black willows bent broke
grey water rippled by eels
as afternoon shifted western wind

in the rain his skin glistened
and his long hair danced into curls
as the rose on the curve
of the shoulder-blade moistened
under patches of frail light
in which we emptied our beer cans

wet we scrambled into the truck
as the broken day bent
like willow boughs into water

I kissed another summer
and despaired for the rose
which would wilt on winter flesh

OROVILLE HIGH, CALIFORNIA

I can't believe I'm eating a cheeseburger
in Oroville, CA, where dogs yelp at ghosts.
What I really can't believe is eating
the cheeseburger in a classroom at Oroville High
among students taught the mastery of printing.
They're ambivalent to instruction,
indifferent to machines which will record
their births and local football games...
machines which are indifferent to Oroville
itself, the buttes beyond the town's
rigid limits where Ishi clawed rock desperately
struggling to preserve his unrecorded songs;
a school where no student knows nor cares
about the almond groves nor the gold
that built Oroville, let alone
Ishi's drum, nor the crisis of extermination,
not even their own.

INUIT

"I wish I kill myself like hell."
—Inuit teen-ager, as reported in
The New York Times, 11/10/79

I write this on barroom walls.
It spells the death of caribou.
I forget we are the eaters of raw meat.

The northern moon freezes on my cheek.
There must be some bird to imitate;
I forget the words of the morning songs.
I will put my ear to the ice...
it remembers.

RENO HILL...LITTLE BIGHORN
June 25–26, 1876

Seven fires form a sacred hoop...
villages circled by people's hands...
not so easily torn apart
by bullets' teeth or cavalry charge
though blood still waters grass.
Reno's retreat buried his dead;
Custer's greed ate his flesh,

and his bones and the bones of his men
whimper in the dark like dogs.
Sitting Bull's children flower spring;
antelope graze these very hills;
fox sniff out mice and loco berries;
wild stallions foal colts
that will prance upon this monument.

Blood enough was spilled...
"It was a good day to die"...
White Bull sang and Crazy Horse.
The war that was lost was won.
Seven fires burn and form
a sacred hoop of people's hands.
Drunken Reno; Custer sired no children.

LISTENING TO LESLIE SILKO TELLING STORIES
New York City, 2/8/79

I take February ice and chill
in stride, enter the subway
to write the various faces
sitting to either side
know children will always listen
as the train shuttles from magic
to Brooklyn

THE SHORT AND THE LONG OF IT

In the Vines

For Oakley in Wisconsin
At Oneida Nation

voices/
he heard voices
painted on the belly of the bridge
over Duck Creek
he knew they were a people/
nation

voices talking of the vines
of wild strawberries
crawling along the creek edge
of the white/pink trilliums
spattering the wood's floor...
snows of spring

a voice urging him to tramp
the ferns and mosquitos of the woods
looking for dinosaur eggs
large as Olmec head sculptures

he knew their haunts/
voices/writings
and we sat below the bridge listening/
listening
and all I heard were the scrawls...
"I love Kim" and "B.I.A. go home"

he asked what they said
he knew they were a people/nation
stranger amongst strangers
perhaps lost/hungry/wounded

how could I explain...
his hands were so fragile
how could I tell him who they were...
he was a spring blossom himself
how could I bring heartbreak
to his fantasy/his boy smile
his six years as he sat anxious
believing and listening
as the berry vines curled
around his ankles and wrists

POSTCARD

Framed
     (Currier & Ives)
     it stands the rigors
of winter
dressed in jackets of snow
settled within the bosom
of the mountains
at the side of a lake

pine aroma
       aging flesh
and aging buildings
one blue and balconied
historic on the hillside street
     (for sale)
caught my eye
      and pause
and I'd coffee at Alice's Restaurant
where I could see the blue
building better
and smell bear and fox
not far beyond
in the mountain wood
in green winter wood
carved out by wind and snow
green as any dream

but the postcard
with many greetings
the emergency hoot
at all hours
sounding fog
(or ship horns of fog)

far from any sea
and the ancient
J.J. Newberry Co.
          the only one
left in the world
probably
dressed holiday
sold funny things
you can't buy in big cities,
or Yum Yum Tree
with chocolate truffles
                  windowed
filling the street
with oh those smells
sweet and tempting and fattening
with Mary's smile and Peg's
candy tease
and the ladies come for tea
to peck at gossip
Norine to smoke
Cathy to coffee
get a look at me
pony-tailed stranger
in a strange country

postcards
I mailed off
          hundreds
to friends and family
          or bears
at Onchiota
          and hawks
          lakes
and burning mountains
leaves like lemon-drops

✳ 224

and limes and dollops of blood
(Deirdre said)
        licked
hundreds of 14 cent stamps
as now I mail off this card

but you can't know
        Yum Yum
        nor Dewdrop
        nor Pendragon
        nor the Java Jive
until you've seen them framed
in their setting,
or the
"good morning, stranger"
as you pay for the *Times*
to get the world news
which you don't need
        anymore
you have become a figure
in the tourist postcard
see, see
        there you are!
leaning against the old hotel
see, see
        the one in blue wool hat
and the blue tennis shoes
you have melted
        like wax
blown into the scene
        blown glass

from the artist's flute
        yes,
"nice to see you"

nice to see that you are
a minute color beneath the gloss
yes, that's you, you
the lady is speaking to you
"have a nice day"
"I'm so happy to see
you in the paper"
Ms. Dudley was wont to say

a line drawn into
      the scene
framed in holiday, festival
      and snow
can't you hear bells ringing
the old man standing
before the downtown library
why, he's ringing bells
bells, bells, bells
before the empty lot
where the movie house was destroyed in fire
(and now rebuilt)

      and snow
falls on his bells
and the ringing ceases
      muffled
is carried off by the winds
or the night descending
thick and dark
on the village
moving slowly onto the lights
as if some great animal
an enormous bear, perhaps
moved out from the winter woods
to enfold you

in dreams
(a dog barks in the town hills
a taxi moves through swirls
        of wind
a lone student ambles down the street
muffler tossed about the throat
its redness brightening the sky
towards laughter throbbing Main Street
the fog horn and a babe wail...
"nice to see you"
the dog barks once more)

        in dreams
is that what it was
a dream, nothing
more than a dream
interlude
(tamarack, cedar, hemlock
dipped in chocolate
        a truffle)
flute notes of wind
blowing through birch boughs
and cedar
        cedar sing over my mother's grave
will it sing to me
over mine
        stranger stalking
        then, now, forever, maybe
the village streets
        winter wind and snow
aroma of pine and bear
chilled to the bone
will cedar sing over mine

as I drop this in the post box

I'm in hopes you will
receive it by Thursday

P.S.
I forgot
to mention
Robert Louis Stevenson
wrote fiction
           (and poems)
here

WALKING WOODS WITH DOGS AFTER A SNOWFALL

A green pristine only a miracle could devise
green color of lake water
billowed in foam
          foam of snow
And, odd, high on a naked tamarack
a banana peel dangles in forest light
some bird will supper

English setters pounce through the banks
noses rutting the fluff
                    tails snapping
against a sapling birch
                    barks echoing

Spruce sags and white pine under snow
                         your
shoulders deep in mystery of thought
end of the year soon to replace holiday

You cannot see the mountains...Marcy or Whiteface
through the green needles, yet they are collecting
winter on shoulders, too
You cannot hear loons
          lakes and ponds frozen to flight
Yet they are there with bear snoring into spring
raccoon plotting the dangling banana peel
deer quietly waiting the setters
          leave
and the crunch of your heavy boots
skunks trailing the scent of dog meat on your hands

Have you dropped bread on the snow for swallows
                    or

your own return
Setters, too, can lose the way in blizzards
as snow covers track and scent while conifers bend
disfiguring the scene you remember these years
of challenging wood and mountain

You have known your way
          always through winter
whatever corridor you stalked
but now in the broad light of this green afternoon
among these green trees, snow covering thin creeks
which yapped like puppies in summer, covering
the dead housecat fox took down months ago
                         there
there, hear it, do you hear it?
the howl? is it wind in the trees, pine
or some spirit of the woods attempting
               seeking
or, is it merely wolf searching its den and young
You shake your head in total disbelief
shake snow off your shoulders
stomp your boots, whistle for the dogs
          time
time to go home in the green light
as it darkens on your face
          green

wind bites your green cheek and smile as you stop
listen to the silence now that the dogs
                    stand
erect tails to the wind as if frozen in frost

You look up
          the banana skin still hangs too high
for raccoon

a bluejay wings off knocking
snow puffs to a fallen log crumbling in age
you must go back to the house
wood to chop for the stove, reports to make
your wife has a plate of cold chicken for a snack
and wild grape jam for a slice of hot toast
                    coffee
so black it will stand your hair on end
You start the return
            think a moment before calling
the dogs, your stance perfectly still
and realize the setters have already reached the backyard
You listen
            the howling has faded into the approaching
                                gloom
pause to catch the scratching of raccoon on bark
fox crunching bones of a bird
or the late flight of summer mallards

Smiles break open
            you drop a glove on the purple snow
sniff, rub the back of your hand against your cold nose
and know there is time
again tomorrow you will walk woods
                with dogs
touch snowflakes with a warm tongue
                listen
fall of light and the hush of darkness
swallowing these green woods
        green
as new spring fermenting in the earth

MYSTERIES

For Tehanetorens

I.

I watched him take down the chicken-wire fence.
His white mane brighter than sun,
His face blue/twilight chicory
as the morning light careened above spruce and pine.
He carried lightness and yet his shoulders drooped;
His hands empty except for a hammer
to pull the mesh away from the garage walls.
He stepped about holding mountains in his hands.

II.

There was nothing left on the shadowed floor
but shadows and a single feather.
Neither a smear nor speck of blood
showed either death or war.
He had cleaned the mess;
brown feathers scattered here and there,
two stuck in the mesh of the wire;
one embedded in the cement wall.
He washed away the blood
except for a stain on his own chin.

III.

His account was brief.
There was no need to garnish that event.
"I came out yesterday morning as the sun
struck the tops of that white pine

traveling east to southward
with a handful of corn.
He'd been a friend...two years.
Two years past we met on the forest floor—
he, drowsy from pain of a broken wing.
Two years I fetched feed and water.
Felt the wing grow in strength,
told him stories and listened as he told stories
to me...his flights across the skies,
the mountain trees, his hours waiting prey
on a lone and naked bough of an elm long dead,
of flights into sky, distant sky of airs and lands
we can't know ourselves. He'd speak
of many mysteries men might need to know
but find them difficult to understand.

"I came out here this morning
glad to know sun would shine today
and no rain fall. A tanager whistled
on that new wood fence across the road
and chipmunks squeaked in the low branches
of these cedars. I think I whistled with the bird.
It was a new day. I'd passed the darkness
of the night once again. A hot cup of coffee
in my hand: my wife put a good breakfast on her table.
I was thinking Jesus had been a real man, and good.
The garage door was open a crack.
Blood smeared the jamb low down
close to the ground. I threw the door open.
The floor was littered with feathers.
A hole torn in the mesh; more blood on the cage floor.
I knew his spirit was in flight
to those mysteries I spoke before. I knew
this raccoon...well, it's natural.

IV.

"Tooth and claw the Christian Bible says.
Somehow I'd suppose it's probably right.
I won't hate the raccoon nor cherish my bird
the less. He struggled to live. More my fault than his,
I put him to death; I signed the paper and paid
the claw and tooth to execute.
What makes me feel bad is that we didn't have
a chance to have a last chat."

V.

Lightness in his hands he carried mountains.
Sun on his mane, his face was dark.
He rolled the wire and dragged it outside
as though it were a heavy stone.
He stacked the 2x4s that formed the cage,
saying they'd make a good fire.
He looked up into the sky.
"I'm mean today. Gotta lot of work to do."

DUGOUT

A Mohawk Speaks to a Salvaged Past

In 1984, when workers drained one of the ponds at a private estate near Malone, N.Y., to repair a dam, two dugout canoes were discovered preserved in the mud. Before they were excavated, leaders at the nearby Akswesasne Reservation were contacted and invited to be present. It is rare for wooden artifacts to survive long in such excellent condition, and carbon dating has revealed them to between four-hundred and five-hundred years old.

Though it has not yet been firmly established which of the Indian peoples then using the region may have built them, the find has distinct archaeological significance for anyone living in the North Country, and especially for the Mohawks of Akwesnase.

Maurice Kenny was present at the excavation. The poem that follows grew out of the discovery and the feeling it engendered in Kenny and other members of the Akwesasne community.

—Chris Shaw

Ancient hollowed canoe discovered in the mud bottom of
Twin Ponds near Malone, New York, in the summer of 1984·

For Salli and Lloyd

rainbows clean the sky
end in the leaves of a pitcher plant
which collects bows and rain
and the plant's bloody flowers
trumpet the morning and storm finishes
clearing the sky, the forest floor
the pond etched by fern and pine

holding a chip of wood no thicker than a sliver,
pond water slurping against tiered banks
and floating logs under the slow flight of coots,
July broke crow's raucous warning, woods opened

235 ✳

to swamp rose, to tamarack, black willow and oak
a rough path through brambles, eryngo, blue flag
and arrowhead; earth wet, bog, rich and dark mystery
...a mere sliver, fat but crumbly in fingers
capable of picking pitcher plant
to heal burnings in the chest...the common cold

silver water ripples decades pass to shore

       sound of stone hammers
       pounding thick log drums woods, echoes down time

quivering in this silver, this sliver, now

       voices: frightening intonation, warning as crow cawed

what is this hair embedded in the gray grain
of this wood—
perhaps hundreds of years—
near 19 feet long, 2 feet wide

egret tells time in the flap of a wing
sweaty labor digging

brown feather floats down from overhead branches
rests upon water turning golden
in this our afternoon, this summer day
eons away, an afternoon which can't hear
egrets or the fall of feathers tipped black
for victory or death

rearing over the water in wind-swell
tuning the tine music of consciousness
awake though dreaming
men rap about trout, fresh water for thirst

cool, delicious

    o, the sky, the woods
    strain as hammers drum hollow the log
    wordlessly chant
    to the beat of sweat slipping into earth
    wordless sounds beginning to float
    air made warm by sun and grebe breast
    ruffled by turtle rising to surface
    frog caught by a foot in the snap

rainbows have cleaned the sky
of storm
for a while, once again

Lloyd heaves, and Steve and Barry,
the dugout is photographed, tethered
now to shore; and Mike holds up freshly caught trout

    breathing is heavy, the tramp along the rim
    of the twin ponds and down wooded hills in the forest

old men should sit in the shade
contemplating grandchildren and songs, what's on the stove
    for his supper
breathing is heavy, history enticed
blood to surge and lungs expand, old
men should be content with rainbows doubling
Akwesasne, rivers with ocean liners, tankers
mountain ponds stand deep in the memory
collective and single—voices shuddered
through egret feathers, bear growls
o, yes, o, remember

in the mud:
bodies forgotten
fingers toes jaw spine

formless words, says a voice

>osprey dive, and deep deep in the woods
bear, fat on summer honey, stands straight
elm could not be taller touching sky
lean to tip a mountain peak, bear stands straight
as an arrow piercing lowering clouds
and a bird-cry brushes leaves of oak
perhaps bluejay or raven
as wolf trots through green shadows
burrowing rabbit as raccoon stands erect knowing
summer can be fatal as arrow rips
progeny, tear of breath and guts left for ants
maggots while tail turns in the wind, poled
or on the cap of a child testing winter

I am the voice
surely there is a story

>wordless, formless windless but sounds
winter and snow is falling
wood is chopped, corn and venison dried
muskmelon stored away in coolness
bear snores in some den

>four men

not those who came to take the boat
return the canoe home

>four men

warrior, prophet, poet, singer

four men

smoke
curls through the chimney into darkness
night, story-teller is ready, now
winter

four men

not those who brought the dugout home

clans, drawn lines between
corn, bean, squash

the men,
warrior, seeker, ambassador, merchant
defender, father, lover, lawyer, hunter
hollow log, dugout ghost returned

cargoing a parfleche of stories
for winter nights when owl sleeps and snow
decorated pine lifting gently in winds
song over fire in the house

absolved;
        resolved
air/drum/water

Get to the story

we believe there might have been four men
the dugout is large enough to safely
comfortably accommodate four men

239 ✳

and four men brought it home

       coyote howls on the hill
       morning is something you cannot squander
       or cap in a little sweetgrass basket
       however red with strawberry

it is a long story
taking many winter nights
maybe four hundred years
maybe five hundred

       there were coots and grebes, mallards and loons
       the loons sang the loveliest
       geese v in precision
       and titmice and woodmice
       remember muskrat, turtle
       wolf howled, dropping pups on mountain sides
       there were coots and grebes
       salmon and trout in each river
       pitcher plant for the common cold
       and her shadow against the sky
       falling, falling

       four men

Tell the story.

       afternoon is something you cannot squander,

the wind blew open the door,
a hush fell heavily upon the room

I knew the great eagle should perch
upon the highest pine...his sight is best

a woman enters, passes a plate of corn bread

I knew the eagle should perch
upon the white pine...it stands the tallest

> leaves have turned golden now, birch maple oak beech
> russet, burgundy...march hawk hunts
> bobcat sleeps on the stout limb of the bending sycamore
> pitcher plant has been picked and stored for winter use
> night not yet a threat
> sun wanders through oak branches
> as though looking for the early moon to rise
> take watch over the darkening woods
>
> hands clenching chicken feathers,
> move in words clothed in ancient tongue
> silent music threads the night
>
> sweetgrass grows around us

wind as though from an eagle's wing fans the room
fire lips in the pot-belly stove, ol'
rabbit dog sniffs, mumbles and sleeps

> here are fish for supper
> words for your mind
> blood for your fire

a face stares through the window, long
hair hangs down the skull, lifts in wind
its cold eyes
stare at the woman,
huddled in a bear robe, her hands clutching greens

Tell the story

twisted, tongue hanging on the chin
splashed in blood
owl awakens though snow still falls
burdens the light

it was a beautiful afternoon
bronzed and reddened
dark clay darkened in the kiln
roped in circles by strong hands
that could slit open the belly of a deer
praised and thanked
with one tug of the knife
it was a beautiful afternoon
coots and grebes, salmon and wood anemones
trembling in the colors, the brilliant colors of the winds
day shimmering like the first day
rainbows sparkling on every drop of dew, prisms
canoe readied we stocked with provisions and furs
and extra moccasins, beaded and resplendent
no sign of thunder, no sign of rain
corn up, we knew it was safe to travel
rivers even now...no more spring floods
past time for strawberries yet too
early for blueberries it was time
four men
father two brothers and an uncle
weapons ready for defense or revenge
presents for any foreigner
skins of water for whatever march, parched corn
dried meat, maple hunks, pheasant feathers
no one knew how long the journey might take
prayer sticks, beaded belts
winds were calm, water smooth
as weathered bone antler rubbed by winter winds
we were prepared

all men *onen*
one trillium bloody red, guards
one vine trails off into the unknowable distance
one jay peeps as eagle ascends to the pine

the story begins

story has long ago begun
it's continuous
in the bear robe warming the old woman's shoulder
in the wolf robe on his husky shoulders
in the turtle rattle held in the other's hand
in the eagle's eye, hawk's scat
story has never stopped

it streams down the handle of the war club
it is caught in the grip of the Great Law
it murmurs in the song of the singer
the pounding of the drum, the arch of the carver
the cry of every child, the poet's pen
the raised foot of each dancer who touches earth
and moves as the squash vine moves, as wind,
it is the ever-widening circle of the village
and the fire in the house
the string of fish caught
the tongues of elk, the belly of moose,
flight of northern geese,
the color of the meadows and meadow flowers,
the sweet berries and the bitter of sumac,
it is the greeting of morning,
it is the hope for a good mind,
story are clouds, grebes and coots
partridge drumming the earth, loons singing,
and where humans heard partridges drum
it is the flow of the rivers, crystal of lakes

it is this canoe, hollowed and safe for journey
it is the mind of humans, the joy of the child
the journey

story has never stopped
a chain of days, night
following night on bat wings, or moons
it is the eastern dawn, the grave on the mountain
it is the mountain. it is time itself whatever time
may be, it is the budding of the beech
and the falling of the leaf, whistle of the wind
it is toothless old men, or old women
who no longer hear, spittle of the sick
it is the fisher at kill, hawk
the birth of groundhog
it is the fire, this fire flaming
in the pot-belly stove stoked
and the ol' rabbit dog asleep beside it
it is the story of nations, nation
and history and circles of the trees
circles

    four men

winter and story move in the ripple

yes, I see, I understand
I will listen, I will listen
      my mother is a turtle
      my mother is a fish
      my mother is a muskrat
      my mother is a beaver
      my mother is a boat
      my mother is a reed
      my mother is my mother

and all her parts are me

my mother is a fish
my mother is a reed
my mother is corn and bean and squash
my mother is sumac and smoke
my mother is honey
my mother is a berry on the bramble
my mother is the sap of the maple
my mother is a boat
my mother is the rapid in the stream
my mother is the wind
my mother is a coot
my mother is a bear
my mother is this house
my mother is the fire
I am my mother and my mother is me

my mother is a fish
my mother is bone
my mother is yarrow
my mother is hawk-weed
my mother is deer
my mother is snipe
my mother is blue heron
my mother is yellow rose
my mother is sprig of mint
my mother is birch
my mother is cedar
that sings in the wind
my mother is cloud
my mother is star
my mother is dream
my mother is grave
my mother is wolf

my mother is water
my mother is loam
my mother is fire
my mother is wind
my mother is fish
I am my mother and my mother is me

and this is the story of four men
who boarded a boat so many years ago
fog has covered footsteps/wind drowned voices

voice: a fingerprint rests upon the wood
etched, a hair still clings
a speck of blood remains, a vibration
stirs the pond, reverberation brushes
the softness of the forest

we're pretty sure it could hold four men

I could feel the sliver quiver on my palm
will I dream tonight
Don't speak of dreams and presences
I hold it firmly on the palm of my hand
and watch it quiver almost turning
I hear
        the sounds of the paddles, water, as wood
        slits through the calm as geese spring

I suggested the eagle

        yes, leaves have turned golden and russet
        march hawk hunts as bobcat sleeps on the stout beech
        the hollowed log, ghost canoe of men
        slithers down water
        silent under wings and sweet gale, silent

as it passes over grayfish, sleek bass, scuds
slinking off from the canoe's wake, silent men
as a dragonfly browses the corners of morning
paddle the swift and quick waters dedicated to motion
directed by need and falling light
to harbor before dark and a meal of parched corn
spirited by necessity to seek home
approval of the elders, of the women
warmth of spouse, laughter of children, bed for exhaustion

is their cargo news or merely pelts
or deer meat from the hunt
is the cargo scalps and victory songs or
the decomposing corpse of a son, friend
bones

Don't ask me what I dream

Don't ask me what I dream
Everytime I dream
I won't remember

Don't forget the pitcher plant
it's growing all over the woods
my mother picks it for the winter

> my mother is fish
> my mother is sky
> my mother is rainbow
>
> my mother is dream
> my mother is drum

bones and shells rattle the dream
blood splattered on the kitchen floor

a car smashed on the highway

Don't ask me what I dream

Smoke trails out the open car window
as we speed toward Malone, the rez

a Greek tanker moves down the St. Lawrence
Cornwall Island is smogged in pollution
Alcoa is getting richer, and Reynolds, and Chevrolet, too
someone plants poplars that won't grow along the river banks
and trees die in the pollution

     my mother is a cedar

     a bear munches suet in the woods
     goldenrod is flowering

     Four men
     reaching home, reaching
     their secret

I suggested the eagle because it has the best eye
I suggested the white pine because it stands the tallest

     their secret message

     Wind rises, river darkens

I'll try to tell their story...

Last Mornings in Brooklyn

SATURDAY MORNING
> Between 7 A.M. and 12 NOON
> Clark Street, Brooklyn Heights,
> Across the street from the Hotel St. George

1.
7 a.m.
I put down Williams' *Paterson*
and pick up the street...
a strange landscape.

2.
The yellow Honda
purrs like a cat
at the curb;
the Korean green-grocer
accidentally
sprays with blue water...
as if a cornflower.
Now it stands quietly
waiting for the driver.

3.
It's a hot day.
A woman sits
on the window ledge
in panties and bra;
her stockings hang drying.
She leans, looks across the street
and asks if I am busy.
I bury my nose in a book.

10.
His t-shirt
cut off

above the belly-button
he contemplates the blue sky
over the street.
His Airedale pulls him forward.

15.
A youth
dribbles
an orange basketball
down the cement sidewalk,
his earphones in place.
The VW bug comes to a shriek.

18.
Apollo and David
strut down
to the health club,
totes on left shoulders,
David misses...
steps where a dog had stood.

22.
Helene pushes Evan's carriage
to the subway door.
She eats a peach, sucking juices.
She waves at all the pigeons.

32.
His hawk feather
straight as a warrior's
he fords into battle,
blonde hair flowing

38.
I know his name is Browning...
no, not the poet;
hurry, he frowns the morning;
his tote-bag is heavy
with thoughts.
Children dance in his head.

40.
Norman Mailer,
Monday through Friday
at nine, safaris
down Clark Street to the subway
newsstand for his *Times*.
Saturdays, I wonder
where he buys his paper.

41.
He stands, he leans, he squats,
he stands again...
casing apartments, looking
for a bill for wine,
waiting for the furniture
to arrive, or his contact, girl-
watching, a child-snatcher? He oils
the imagination.

TEKONWATONTI: MOLLY BRANT

I, TEKONWATONTI

I, Tekonwatonti
child of these rivers
girl of this wood
woman-to-be of this house
this bed of branches
gathered for my husband
to be woman of this pot
of mortar and pestle
of fields of corn
brambles of berries
of gathered faggots
to warm his thighs
of breasts swollen with milk
for suckling children
and full of stories for winter nights

pleased to love, happy to birth
honored by a good man
will become, at peace, my mother
whose bones eventually
will be enjoyed by wolverine

I, Tekonwatonti
whisper the sounds of my name
to the voices of the night and the waters
that we women, the grandmother of the night
and my sisters in the fields of the sun
labor the birthing of generations
of muskrat, loon, raspberry, tamarack,
and the differing cries of cubs
to break open membrane
and be counted

I,
I,
Tekonwatonti, I
no, we
children of these rivers
girls of these woods and meadows
kissed by the warmth of Grandmother Moon
nourish the mouths, bellies of our men...
the Great Turtle, *Tarachiawagon,*
and the powerful giant, *Shagadyoweh,*
we women dig the flint and smooth the arrow
happiness in our hands
that we, too, community the village
and populate our future

corn whispers the fields
as winds surge the dawn

MOLLY BRANT TO WILLIE

They believe I bewitched Catherine
and her children of your loin
by painting designs on their thighs
which damn them barren.
They believe I have spelled my brother,
Joseph, so that he will wield a hatchet
into their blonde heads,
a cry on his curled lip as he sucks
blood and chews a naked heart.
They believe I prayed their corn
wither in August fields,
their skinny cows diseased,
their cabins burned crisp
by marching Caughnawagas
bent on destruction, in league with the French.
They believe I can stop the wind,
halt the rapids of a river,
turn the sun into the moon, poison air.
They believe my potions draw
love circles around your feet,
tether your heart to my moccasins.

I am a girl...waiting with a cup of tea,
waiting in the cold bed across the long night.
I could not harm the mouse that steals your cheese,
nor darn your sock lest you pain
from the bump of thread beneath your toe.

SIR WILLIAM'S REPLY TO MOLLY

Yes, I laugh.
True, you are a witch, alchemist
of September apples, red and savory
in the bin of the springhouse;
you are the bite of cider,
the bitter of bush cranberries,
the smart of fire rising under
your kitchen kettles; and the touch
of your small hands, a balm
that drives off storms rearing
in the brain of this aging man
weary of state and war, of constant
separation between my lips, your breasts.
Your adoring, William.

MOLLY: REPORT BACK TO THE VILLAGE

"Leg
          blackened at the stump with blood
Fingers
          scattered through brush
Torso
          painted and jeweled
                    porcupine quills
                    pretty beads
beads rolling off in a line
                    ants
scurrying from a foot
torso split open a ripe pumpkin
entrails
          hang/drip from rib cage
                    belly

Swath of black hair
                    blue
          from clouds and river water
                    three feathers stir in the breeze
The head...
          missing
                    kicked off into the brush
                    a ball

Name
          unknown/unsung
          there are many
                    too many

Buzzards wait in the sky

Why do they call this the Indian war?

It isn't Indians who want rivers
and land and more pelts to ship to kings,
or throats to pour whiskey down.

Why?
This is my report. That is all. *Niaweh.*"

GENERAL JEFFREY AMHERST

"The Crown will reign.

Johnson will dangle by an earlobe.

Painted savage.

Johnson, indeed, naked and vile
        in the sight of God and King.

Has he no shame? That squaw
        beneath his buttocks.

May God save him from this madness,
        or the devil take his spleen."

SIR WILLIAM JOHNSON: ON HIS DEATH BED

Catty, Catty who?
My wife?
My wife is Molly, Brown Mary.

Oh! Yes, the servant girl
I bought those years back.
The German from the Flats.
Indentured.
Yes, she bedded in my bed,
suckled my son,
and hid in the closet
when gentlemen and ladies
came to sup or tea.
Not very bright, as I remember.
Yes, I did take her to marry...
her twenty-fifth birthday...
that long night she died.
She kept a clean house
and snot from her child's chin.
I dignified her bed and breast.
I placed a copper ring upon her finger
and took shame from her cheek.
The least I could do.
Poor Catherine, poor Catherine.

Bury the remains
of my beloved wife, Catty,
next to those of mine.

(Molly, oh Molly...forgive me.)

MOLLY: AT HIS DEATH

Kwaaaaaaaaaaa...

My hair streams in the river,
chips of my flesh shrivel under the sun,
the nub of my little finger
is buried in the earth with his bones.

Kwaaaaaaaaaaa...

I have no arms to hold me
no cheek against my own
no might to protect my house
or the limbs of my children.
Who will hunt for my pot?

Kwaaaaaaaaaaa...

Eight times I spread my legs
and gave him his flesh.
Twenty-one years we lay
thigh by thigh under summer stars.
How do I pull grass over his face now?

Kwaaaaaaaaaaa...

MOLLY

I wish never to live to see
            another war.
I've gagged on flesh
            and choked on blood.
I've seen the bones of my brothers
            float in the river,
smelled the stench of their rot.
My nostrils are clogged
            with powder smoke.
My arms are weary from the
            weight of rifles.
Villages are burned to the ground,
old men pierced on stockade posts.
Women and babies sleep on the
            scars of bayonets.
Maggots infest the bed.

General George, town destroyer,
            you have won.
Won and accomplsihed more in your
            victory
than you ever dreamed.
Our blood is your breakfast.
The flames of our village smoke
            the ham you carve and bring to your lips.
General George, leader of a new
            country,
our stars are yours now,
but our blood stains your flag.
Remember we were once
            powerful, a formidable nation
now on our knees.
Your hatred controls

our destiny.
May your nation never know
    this unbearable loss, this pain,
    this exodus from home, the smoking
    earth,
    the sacred graves of the dead.

I bathe in this river to wash
    away the blood of war.
    But no water can
    wash away
    the horrors tattooed
    on my flesh.

I pray I shall never smell
    the cannons of war again,
    nor hear the cries,
    nor see the body of a chief
    mutilated by hate and fear
    and greed.

As your stars, General George, rise
    above the many battlegrounds
I want you to remember all those
    who died
so that your flag may wave
    in tribute.

CALL ME...WOMAN

New Amsterdam, 1652

They were so many and we were so few.
Pigs were allowed to eat the rotting fruit
heaped on the grass; their own children
played games, throwing them in sport.

I have come a long way...call me woman.

Corn failed that year, drought took beans;
no deer, as they had cleared the woods.
Only pigs and rats brought on their ships.
Pigs kept the winter stomach warm;
their rats were poisoned.

I have come a long way...call me woman.

My uncle hung from the elm in the square
for taking a pig to roast above his fire.
My cousin sewn into a leather bag—
first beaten with rods, sodomized
at the muzzle of Nicolaes Hildebrant's pistol,
was tossed in the river.

I have come a long way...call me woman.

My blood flows through their history...
they cannot deny my place though
my name was canceled and my flesh left to rot
under the peach tree with the fallen fruit.
today my blood still flows in the pools
and springs below the cemented earth,
but Van Dyck's peach orchard has long been axed.

I have come a long way...

My cry of hunger and my children's cries
are heard at the fountain in Bowling Green.
Even the British could not wish it away.
My dreams are in the mountains, my dreams
flow in the great rivers, and rise again
and again each spring with the blood-
red strawberries of the meadows.
My children still dance the summer corn
at Akwesasne, Onondaga, Cattaraugus;
my sisters plant corn and braid baskets;
my brothers hunt and fish and lead us
into the future where there are no Dutch.

I have come a long way...call me woman.

My blood is everywhere. You can see it
on the sun, taste it on the peach,
hear it on the river, feel it on the cheek.

I have come a long way...call me woman.

My death cannot be denied, nor my name canceled.

ON SECOND THOUGHT

FOR BRETT

He spotted them
committed a cermonial
dance
around them,
knelt
leaned
wet his lips
pressed
the trigger
and shot.

Click and for a very
long time
the black-eyed
susan
would gloss
on the paper
and perhaps
never
wither
into autumn.

He had leaned
into
something
precious,
something
inexplicable
complex.

RECUERDO

"...whistles kept blowing, and the dawn came soon."
—Edna St. Vincent Millay

smile on the rain
reflected in the window
we both shot looks
into the pane and hurt
rolled tears down
glass flesh and mouths
hugged empty nights
of West Village shadows
lurking like boys in dark
doorways filling with rain
splashing your cheek
and my school books

nothing accomplished
but the smile on the rain
and the mouths closed
as our siamese body
nothing accomplished
but that was enough
we knew our tongues

our lives cleaned left
Christmas in our hands
and strawberries asleep
on thighs we kissed
and split the echo
of our moans
in the ticking clock

SUNFLOWER

Three summers
it grew
near the black river
beyond the raspberry
brambles
at the bottom of the hill.

The morning walk
always assured
it would be there.

Last spring
wanton boys
found its stalk.
Summer
this July
will be partially
empty.

They will come back
for the raspberries,
too.

ON THE JETTY

El Morro on the Pacific Shore

Consumed by consummation
black wings rose from the seas,
entwined their feathers with the dawn
striking the bulwark of piled rocks.
The wet sun twisted over the horizon
as iron wave after wave struck,
cleaned intrusion from the stones
lifted the moment and the thrill
into the patterns of morning
and wings joined pinions
while day sprang into its usual place.

COMMON DAYS

SPRING

a boy
a girl...
          students
lean against the hill
facing Mt. Baker
reading a book
          together...
Houseman's
Shropshire poems

MICHAEL

bounding footballs
on the hillside
near Cedar
his hockey leg
in a cast,
his Mohawk smile
firmly planted
on lips in autumn sunshine

          Van of students
                    singing
          their lost way
          down the mountain slope
          towards
          a poetry reading

My Lynn (W)

deep
in daffodils
black-eyed susans
johnny jump-ups
and rows like hedges
of cherry
tomatoes
ripening
now on the bough
she stretches
toward the sun
watering
her children
while Bisbee,
the dog,
waits the flowering
of the evening
moon

WILDFLOWER

The throat
of a peanut butter jar
clutches a fistful
of black-eyed-susans
erect before the glass
window magnifying
the high wooded hill
behind. One blossom
stretches on a single leg
reaching for the sun
as it darkens; birch silvers-
foil caught in a last ray.
Such simplicity must
not go unnoticed.

ABOVE THE SARANAC
A Painting

For Lorne

Mallards splash under willows;
black-eyed susans and wild
harebells sway the meadow
in a breeze. Under noon,
July filters river waters,
glistens heavy silver on the ripples.
A young man in wet purple shorts
fishes the flow, his line
attracting trout, his bare
shoulders teasing the sun
to ravage his flesh.
Behind, on the hill raspberries
redden on canes
spraying over a stone wall.

GHOSTS

Just up the road
Bartok
cottaged
with notes and clefs
on his staff

listen, on a quiet
summer eve
you might
hear
him
over
the buzzing
of mosquitoes'
play

"SULA"

the cat
left
winter on the rug

now the couch
is downed
with fur

it must
be
spring

IN THE TIME OF THE PRESENT

NEW SONG

We are turning
                eagles wheeling sky
We are rounding
                sun moving in the air
We are listening
                to old stories
Our spirits to the breeze
                the voices are speaking
Our hearts touch earth
                and feel dance in our feet
Our minds in clear thought
                we speak the old words
We will remember everything
                knowing who we are
We will touch our children
                and they will dance and sing
As eagle turns, sun rises, winds blow,
                ancestors be our guides
Into new bloodless tomorrows.

PHOTOGRAPH
Carlisle Indian School (1879-1918)

For Geary Hobson and Paula Olinger

I hear ancient drums in the eyes
see dances on the mouth
* * *

why is this teenage boy
stiff in the shutter
punishment, pain on the cheek
loss in folded hands
* * *

who is this boy...nationless
non-descriptive in an army uniform
devoid of hair-feather, fetish and paint
* * *

stiff young sapling rising from some eastern wood
straight as a Duwamish totem
tall as a southwestern mesa pueblo
collar so tight it proclaims a hanging
no pemmican or jerky or parched corn
in the clenched fist that your mother
gave to eat on the road to Pennsylvania
where Delaware once built Longhouses
made fires, loved in furs, fished rivers
praised the Creator for boundless beauty
* * *

who is this boy...hair cut, tongue cut
whose youthful warrior braids lay heaped
          on the barber's floor
spine straightened by General Pratt's rules of order
* * *

ancient image scattered over forested hills
so many leaves from a dying apple tree

***

who is this teen-age lad with eyes cold
            in utter fear
mouth vised and shut of prayer and song
whose thin legs tremble within the army trousers
arms quiver in dread of the unexpected
(an instructor standing off from the flash
of the insensitive camera demanding compliance)
***

there should be a flute to his lips
making songs, music of love
there should be a lance in his grip to take home game
there should be a future on the roll of his dark cheek
there should be a vision quest in his spirit
a name given for honorable deeds
a drawing of the deed on stretched skin
            of the winter count/calendar
***

he stands before the photographers
amalgamated in uniform and shaved head
he stands compromised before his teachers
all that is left to him which is him...
beaded moccasins below the cuffs of his pants
but the bead work so faint in the photo
his great Nation cannot be fathomed
(it can be guessed that probably the supply room
ran out of army shoes the morning
his wagon arrived at the boarding school)
***

who is this lad
he has no name.
no land.
no Nation.
Is he Jim Thorp. Louis Tewanima.
Where was he born. When was he born.

287 ✳

Who was his father. His uncle. His siblings.
Who was his mother who suckled him at breast.
Is this boy entombed in the unmarked grave
          of the Military Institute
which won so many wars by bringing
so many proud children to their young knees.
* * *

I listen for the drum in your eyes
wait to see the dance on your mouth
all I hear are your bitter cries
          of anguish
* * *

He has no name
only a reflection
* * *

his is one of the many spirits
Chief Seattle prophesied
would forever roam this once
free and beautiful land
and that always the General Pratts
would be aware of the ghosts.
* * *

this photograph...
a reminder
of this nameless boy
who is he...
my grandfather

Roman Nose: Cheyenne Warrior

Killed at the Battle of Beecher Island
September 17, 1868

Warrior, where your pony pranced on your mother's breast
Grey cities rise to break the sky;
Cheyenne, where your father sang in Almighty's sun
Rivers flood and cottonwoods wither.

Ripe plums hung in the afternoon.
The Father waited;
Dark plums hung in the twilight,
The Father waited.
Blood fell from the tree of his body
While the Father waited.
In the blue dusk at the river's edge
He sighed and rolled his eyes:
The Father looked down
And sucked his breath.

> Women cried and slashed their wrists;
> Women cried and cut their hair;
> His pony was led to slaughter;
> Women cried and gashed their legs.

Grass grew between his teeth,
Grass grew through his fingers;
Streams flowed from his lips;
Deer came from his breast;
A wolf howled upon his cheek;
A bear hunched on his eyelids;
Grass grew between his teeth, and birds came:
Bats, hawks, kingfishers,

Eagles flew down to his scaffold, and crows.
Youths blew into flutes.
Grass grew through his fingers.

      Drums stilled,
      Rattles shook,
      Dancers
      Pantomined in fire light.

They covered his flesh with ripe plums,
They covered his flesh with hide,
Wolf came, the deer,
Buffalo came, bat came,
His arms were two arrows,
His legs were two lances.
From the dust of his loins
Rose a cottonwood and it flowers the plains

      Father, take his horse;
      Father, take his arrows;
      Father, take his feather;
      Father, take his anger.

Over the grass that grew between his teeth
A nation marched;
Over the grass that grew through his fingers
Buffalo passed, elk, wild peas passed
Into the dust of his groin;
The ancient lands once covered with grass
Blazed fire,
Charred under the sum.
Under swords,
Under cattle and wheat.

      Winds swept off the mountains

Blew his feather, his breath,
Blew the dust of his mother...
Nothing lasts long but rocks...

Warrior, the iron has rusted upon the earth;
Cheyenne, the useless grass is trampled;
Cattle diseased, the sheep hungry;
Warrior, gold has been spilt from the mountains!

The scars of your children shine and burst in the east;
The morning door of the lodge is closed;
Warrior, a boy climbs the knoll to dream;
Cheyenne, the fire waits to be lighted
In the ashes of the grey cities, the wheat.
You did not die for nothing...
It was a good day to die
Under the plums, the eagle's flight.

O
RAIN-IN-THE-FACE

       Lakota warrior
don't you wish you had
torn out Custer's heart
       with your angry hands
and eaten it raw
       without salt
as ol' Whittier claimed
in the same poem which you sold on the Coney Island Boardwalk
between bottles of booze
and starvation
       for home in the Dakotas.

O
Rain-in-the-face
I've wished a million times
to eat the bloody hearts of enemies
gorging hunger, appeasing anger
as I sell my poems across the nation
from the steps of Greyhound buses,
or in those indifferent halls of ivy
that would be happier if I, too,
       sold at Coney Island.

I've been looking at your picture-
postcard on the wall over my typewriter
for a lotta years
the eagle feather standing in the long hair
the satisfaction on your lips
       as though you were pleased
with Whittier's lie
as though you had eaten Custer's heart
       as it quivered in your hand.

Successful revenge is a good feeling
I've thought this a long time
but who do I want revenge against
                and for what?

Who is my enemy?
I have eaten my own heart many times
and eaten the heart of crow, the heart of the sun
but I wear no eagle feathers, I am no warrior
and sometimes think I have no starvation
                for home
no Dakota lands
                no home
there isn't a bear in the mountains
that would move over and offer its cave
nor hawk which would fit me into its nest
and I have never eaten hawk or bear.

Soon Greyhound will growl me across America again
                to your Dakotas
                Will I find earth there,
                a heart
waiting to be torn apart in my teeth
swallowed and digested by belly acids?
Everyday I seem to face a battle
                at some Little Big Horn,
gun shots all around and bloodied faces
spring up from coulees,
war cries and death cries
                assault my ears
and I plunge teeth into warm flesh.

O
Rain-in-the-face
I understand why you sold the poem
to the hordes milling the boardwalk at the sea
                at Coney Island.

MASK

He stands there at the edge of pines
He grins though missing a tooth
His hunter's cap, his red-checked jacket
smelling of the hundreds of hunts.
He stands at the edge...
he will always stand there
as long as I sleep in dreams.

I smell his coat, it smells of deer, venison,
grouse and pheasant. A spatter of blood
rides his right cheek, his left hand holds a rifle,
the right tugs on a line of bloody game,
rabbits mama will stew for supper,
sew the fur into winter mittens, or muffs.

He stands there at the edge of pine...
darkness and quiet drops behind him.
He offers no words yet smiles,
eyes twinkle. I need to hear his words
warm in the now evening air. I need
his gift of words, images for me to slip
deeper into the sleep of comforting dreams.

His figure moves into the woods,
the darkness of the pine. He lifts his gun;
he drags his line of bloody rabbits.
I shout for him to wait.
He stops, turns, beckons me to follow.

I wake, knowing he will return...
another dream, another night,
another time when I need
the death, the blood of his wild game.

One dream one day he will speak and not
just beckon me to follow him into the woods,
dark but heavy with autumn and falling
leaves of winter, he will come again.

THE HANDS OF ANNIE-MAE AQUASH

For Camie and Elizabeth...
women of courage and conviction

I. 1976

Out of dark Dakota cold and snow
they rise finger by fingertip
inked in blood to print on skulls,
indelibly, of those who own no heart;
drawn from ancient wells of a million veins...
blood close to the skin surface.

Hands cut at the wrists by foreign
tricksters, masters of medieval
torture who school the world in
depravity, masters starved for flesh
and broken bones, strive to keep breath
in Salem and the ax hot from human pain.

II. 1989

Child of old America
Girl of fervor
Youth of freedom
Woman of conscience

Annie-Mae, what good are my tears,
sorrow; watching the camera move
across snows and shadows of the hour.
Rage blinds sight of what action to take
as I home Oklahoma now.
Temporarily this autumn eve of October...
in the hall whispering your vision,

resounding the language of your voice.
Students, heads bowed in shame
in the horror, too startled by your murder
to protest. They have seen Sand Creek, My Lai
and now the massacre of you, mind
raped and spirit, head crushed after
gun shot, hands severed at the wrists
for their duty packed in sawdust
and shipped to the capitol for further contamination.

III.

All you ever wanted was milk in your breasts
for the children; corn and rabbit
for the generations; cleanliness
for the earth for naked feet to touch
while dancing on the belly of their mother;
freedom from want...is that so much to ask;
respect for a grave, respect for a prayer,
respect for the first moon and the first sun
rising slowly over turtle's back.

Rage is not sufficient.

IV.

I kiss those severed fingers one by one
hoping to suck out your courage
and defiance, your strength as seed
to replant, harvest, to nourish
the very young of the people, all people.

Finger by fingertip I kiss the flesh
and suck your blood which spurts

from your life...as long as drums bang
and songs remain the essence of human-kind.

I lay the eagle prayer feather
on your figurative grave,
knowing well, rage is not enough
nor revenge satisfactory.

MOOD PIECE

Rising in sunset colors
it embraced the shoulders
of the mountain
crushed in snow
spiked by green pine and spruce.
It rose,
shadows swallowed the valley
until at its zenith
pearl
new as morning milk
steaming from a pail
it burst a rocket
showered the iced lake
with sparkles,
sky illuminated
the underside of a desk lamp
and the world was better
for the moon's course across the night.

Writing a Love Letter I Know You Will Never Receive

At two P.M. Brooklyn is a pile of grey slush
this January 12...day before Friday the 13th.
I can't avoid the 4th floor window;
                    xmas trees
sparkle across the street in the Hotel St. George
as though co-ops believed Christmas was every day
(not in Brooklyn, for sure);
                    pretty faces
hurry in the falling afternoon...some
to the health club down the street with their totes
flapping against straight backs above melon buttocks...
                    longing to be healthy;
                    shopping bags
start from Sloane's supermarket chock-full
of groceries; others a collection of rags
and dented dreams which forced my sentimentality,
and I suck chocolate-chip cookies wondering
when to get out my own plastic bags
and consider what I'd carry: Shakespeare
or Maugham, Black Elk or Dickens, Villon
or Bukowski; a mug, hot plate, Rolaids and deodorants?
To be urban is detrimental;
                    careers flatten
if you live in a city. *Friend*, they say
What's a Mohawk living in a big city for?
                    They forget
Pueblos were the first apartment dwellers,
that Mohawks built most of these skyscrapers
threatening heads; they forget we always lived
in villages from where we could take
an easy stroll to the cornfields or blackberry patch,
or fish trout in a cold stream and certainly not far
                    from the mountains.

You can pray in Brooklyn, climb
to the highest stanchion of the bridge, or on the shores
of Coney Island, or in the rumble of the streets,
or at your window when dawn drives off darkness.

I wish I had a nickel for each hour I've sat at this
                        window,
or just those hours thinking about you,
or El Salvador, or Rain-in-the-Face.
Have you any idea of how many letters I've written
sitting in this window...of thanks, begging,
congratulating, appreciating, scolding, proselytizing,
                        or whatever.
Now I am writing a long letter to you I know
you will never get to read...like other love letters
                I never send.
                I write them
                on air
or on the windowpane and the words vanish as the sun sets
over Newark, New Jersey, never to be read, nor filed
                away,
                nor published
when I am dead. I write them anyway; these raps...
                as Billy
                would have said,
these raps to worlds that haven't time to listen...
                ears waxed
                to love.

"WHY IS SCARFACE YOUR FAVORITE MOUNTAINS?"

Asked by Ralph Etienne

Not just because
I see its shoulders
from my window
towering
above the iced lake,
or it holds winter pine,
spring and trilliums.
The scar reminds me
of eons of wounds:
a broken lupine,
an aged wolf,
the Iroquois woman
who perhaps lost
a husband hunting
or son on the vision quest,
night stars which dazzle,
winds which sweep the earth,
all the pains of darkness,
and the children who dream
to climb its heights.

SWEAT

bathtub
might well
run red
like an
Indian's scream

the knife sits
close to the dirty
water

feet and calves,
thighs and testicles
dare to slide
into the depths
of hell
observing the Ivory soap
float

framed flowers
from Geronimo's
Oklahoma grave
the tub in triumph
and
Paul's
pink waterlily
still floats
in the photograph
and is the reminder
of so much death

the room is freezing
from the steam
rising out

of the waters

the foot lifts
the toes smile
to see there are still
five

you remember
Hilary, a Jew,
hid in the closet
upstairs
from Hitler
double bolting the door
from the inside

this should be sufficient
to soothe and change
waves of thought
the wave of scalding
water lapping
first the testicles
then nipples
at the edge

lie still
and the glossy waters
will reflect
the tears
caught
consuming
history and old age

"Is there a doctor
in the house!"
As there is no view

from this tub

smell sweet
strawberries
of June
scent the delicate
iris
blooming on the creek shore

red screams
grow louder
echoes
beneath the waters
in unexplored
channels

a bubble floats
Chief Pontiac
the French
mad with Revolution
and Jim Morrison.
The blood rises
the knife clatters
to the floor

steam of sweat
envelopes
the entire space

PIMA

Eyes of desert night
word/tongue peaches of Arizona
orchards planted by old women
praising as I praise your mouth,
eyes behind shadows.

Pima, your beauty touched
I quiver, store words in a basket
as women store fruit,
and your smiles of autumn
on a bar stool in Brooklyn.

You flee via Pan-American
to blooming cactus, silence.
Desert afternoon will fire
your flesh, mine
cools with morning.

DANCING AT ONEIDA NATION
Brenda's Gift

She shook, shook, shook;
beans maybe, pebbles possibly,
rattle, rattle, rattle—
or rice, but probably corn
from one metal colander
to another all the time
her feet slowly lifting, lifting
from the wood floor dropping, dropping
down again onto the planks
which pulsed from her dance.

She said nothing as she worked:
shaking, shaking the pans, rattling.
Her shoulders to my gaze,
I watched her hips move in time—
rhythm of green corn swaying
on a July morning breeze.
Wisconsin was in her hips,
Indian in her rattle as dried
kernels rolled around the sieved pans.
Music of the Longhouse volumed the kitchen.

Her ceremony near complete,
she hunted out a plastic bag
and poured the colander's music
into it then wrapped it in a purple
cloth and tied the bundle with hide.
Only then did she turn and face...
my eyes still hearing the magic
of the rattle and felt the gentle
dance of her hips and moccasined feet...
and she held out the purple sack
to my hands, a bundle of corn
ready to pop over a fire.

AN AMERICAN NIGHT

"...a large eye/opened in the side of the mountain."
from "Secret Agent," by Barbara A. Holland

Moonlight kissed black-eyed-susans
as bear trotted the mountain road;
wild though indigenous things stole
the hour: raspberries ripening under
July moon; bobcats at suck; deadly night-
shade sprawled along a broken fence;
at the junction a lone hiker, yellow band
around his head, pisses down
into a gulch while listening to flailing
prayers of a run-away minister
purple in sin of theft from the country
parish hunting and thrashing brush
for coins that had tinkled
that morning in the collection
basket; off in the woods, deep
and tangled with witchhobble,
a tall man holds a gun against
a boy's temple as his naked girlfriend
twists in undergrowth, sumac and red
willow; raccoon claws up the beech
trunk; on sandy shingled shore
the moon-sheened lake reflects
writhing flesh, glistening and moaning;
a child cries in a lean-to cabin; one great
virgin pine pushes at the stars and
a thrush sings...fears a lumberjack;
luna, luna of the summer vision.
We cannot blame the moon, children's
old grandmother...only the shine
which leads the way, what sun disfigures
in dawn's eye.

CHRISTMAS

a tatty plastic wreath
hangs lopsided
in the door window

she sits up close
to the woodstove
(neighbors have piled
wood high near the wall)
sucking the thin
heat into her chattering bones

an empty paper plate
of "meals on wheels"
has been licked clean

she works, intricate
weavings of black ash
splints to baskets
with rheumatized fingers
knuckled up marbles

she smiles down
on something
which
has come to visit
she speaks to the mouse
as if it were a cat
or granddaughter
she never had the luck to birth

she hums as she works
in a language
now strange to the world

of Leno and the Bundys

keeping time
she stamps her feet
from both cold
and the rhythms
of her ancient song

she laughs at the cold
loneness, the lump
at her wrist, the spring
which may arrive
she laughs at the cracks in the walls
which show the lights of her life
the chinks of death
foretold in the passing

THE NOTE

Michael Dorris

This grey April noon will pass.
There will be sun under which
old leaves can be raked into piles
and the lawn will be dressed
for summer parties, lilacs will bloom
after hyacinths. Peace. Peaceful
at last. But clouds must move
out of the dream which kept me awake
most of the night. Juxtaposition,
enigma raise ugly heads. I tried to read
River City, the magazine.
I tried to read my own new poems.
Yes, I should have read *Playboy*.
I counted books, videos,
the individual hairs on my legs.
Perhaps I'd been better off if I had stuck
to the traditional...sheep.
My God, life will go on...hikes,
birth showers, barbeques, weddings,
and more deaths than Edna St. Vincent Millay
could shake a stick at or write poems about.
Desperate thoughts demand desperate actions.
One cliché after another cliché.
Where is the metaphor in all of this?
I'd suppose a simile is more apropos.
I find images scattered throughout the dream,
on this page, in the subconscious.
On the fantasy walls with Tarzan, the Ape Man,
with Dick Tracy, and the Nutcracker.
My dream was haunted by Charles Ives'
America...metamorphosed
into a nightmare. OK. I am literary.

If Matthew Arnold can get away with it
why can't I...to make a point.
It is not like loading this with
the tragic deaths of Black Kettle,
Captain Jack of the Modoc, Pontiac,
Crazy Horse, William of Canajoharie or
Lorne Simon. I am trying to make
a point, perhaps numerous points
in writing this without the solid subject
I teach writing students
they must use: a plastic bag, a mouth
of marbles, jar of applesauce,
a sandal of sand, and be wild.
M period; D period, M.D.
M.D. means doctor of medicine.

We must be wild, the last grip
possible, the last breath. Ruthless,
wild, abandon ourselves to the sun.
No, the sun has not opened its petals today.

All night I lay in dreams thinking of this,
remembering the night I brought the knife
into the scalding waters of the bathtub
and later claimed that action to be a sweat.
I wished to drown in bloody waters
and be at peace. Peaceful at last. Peace...
I had committed no sin. I had not shot
Abraham Lincoln nor dug a hole in Custer's ear,
nor kidnapped the Lindbergh child.
Innocent. I plead innocence.
I don't buy *Playboy*.
So why am I dreaming this stuff.
I confessed my crime in the bloody waters
of my bathtub where the Ivory soap

floated, skimmed the surface of peace
within my own bosom. I confess
nothing but the surprise in this
line-break. And I assure you I regret less.
Bury me in the pauper's grave...a scaffold...
My spirit is wretched in the nothing
of nothingness. My being is
translucent as the scales of the salmon
which once swam the rivers of my homelands.

I absolve myself. I am free,
wild, ruthless in this confession,
in this note I leave for the *Times* to print.
Pinch my arm. I shall squawk.
I am very much alive.
The dream last night which sucked
my very spleen has passed into an
atavistic moment and dropped into Jung's lap.
And he may have the pleasure of sorting it all out.
My countenance is serene, but the clipping
may be set afire with a match.
My heroes, we have nothing to fear.
The lawn needs attention.
I'll decorate it with metaphors
and snippets of Ives' rendition
of *America*. Goodbye Michael, farewell...
And may the flowers forgive you.

TEKONWATONTI: AUGUST 1777, GERMAN FLATS

A lost poem

I don't remember...
are there forget-me-nots, bee-balm,
vervain, wild onion. I know
hawkweed burns and flames near my house.
Little house, hut...a far cry
from the mansion William
and I built at Johnstown.
Well, that's spilled milk now.
Shed no tears. There's a future
to be considered, a war won, children
fed and protected by stout arms. More
to worry about than this hut
of a house. I mustn't be selfish...
so much depends on common sense...
but I'm feeling like the indentured
servant his poor Catty was more every day
than mistress of a mansion.
Servant. Pawn. Idiot. And fool.
No tears. Be strong. Resilient. Tough.
Use your intelligence, your head.
Look at that fragile forget-me-not,
or that single iris standing
along the shore of this creek
to such indifferent eyes but mine.
Who cares. The iris does.
And so should I.

Molly Brant (Tekonwatonti) lived temporarily in German Flats after the death
of her husband Sir William Johnson. His son, John, disregarded his father's will
and evicted her from Johnson Hall, the mansion they had shared. Catty was
Johnson's first wife and John's mother.

ESSENCE

I am the blood of this grass
which feeds maggots that
will consume my flesh.
I will return to the field
and my blood will feed
the red berry ripening under spring.

Grass are my eyes
and I view into the years
of desolation out of ruin.
The blood will spill on rock
dry winds will sweep
its red dust into space.

My eyes are crows
who laugh in the early
of morning slanting across elm
boughs which have no
right to grow in mountain soil.

Crows are my black wings.
Crows are white winter.
Their caw is darkness.
The darkness is the ebony rose
that wilts in the summer hand.

The hand is the receptacle of blood.
From these fingers cries
of creation stream...hawk,
berry, the pine, trout
of old mountain creek.

My mountain is the mystery

of all seasons...now thick
in snow, cold to noon.
pink of falling light
striking bare tamarack
and rusting cedar.

Cedar is where my mother
sleeps; her bones brittle
and cracked by rod and spade.
She will never pick berries again,
nor kiss my father's lips.

Berries are blood
thinning in veins.
I will eat grass, gain
strength to combat
maggots buried in muscles
of my thighs.

My father will step out
from snow, create
summer of December.
He will replace the grass.

UNCOLLECTED POEMS

VISITING ELAINE

Sitting at her kitchen table, Fredonia, New York

Now white berries
in the cold of winter
have fallen
soon
blackberries
will dangle
in the warmth of summer
sweet and moist

Old snow
under March arbor
spring burns though all limbs
begins to move
through vines
up arms
lifting through earth

Sun slants
the hill
tickling white pines
the forgotten tomato garden
goldfish pond
where a yellow cat
waits for the fish—
first snap of its tail

Patches
of shadows
in the backyard
falling against
rubber tires
an old green car

flower stalks so dry
they are indistinguishable
a flagpole
lilac bushes
aching to be free
of melting winter
and burden of cold

O, I feel spring
on the cheek
as sunlight
lifts and falls
across the skin
while walking the long wide lawn
crunching winter tatters

Rags and remnants
an old tom creeps the backyard
out of dark winter
a mole rushes across dead grass
a raven wheels high above the black river
the smell of raccoon is on the bark of spruce
daffodils are not far behind

Walnut ice cream at midnight
coffee at dawn
biscuits and gravy for breakfast
at the Alley Cat Cafe
newspapers at noon
a bus ride to the big city
reading poems to strangers
always ride back in the dark
on the western Thruway

Did they pick all the peppers

did they dig the cache of potatoes
did they remember the long melon vines
fruit rich and ripe to a boy's tongue
did they remember the stalks of celery
the green beans onions carrots
eggplant cabbage and the many herbs
Did they make it through the month of January
Did they save the seeds

Listen, my friend, the sap bubbles
        in the maple
crocus stir in the softening earth
rabbits have vacated burrows
I hear a peeper in the white pine
see bluejay preening in the elm
I watch the metal of a spade and hoe
        glisten under sunlight
and smell manure steaming against the barn
it won't be long now
I watch it grow through the kitchen windows

GOING TO THE MOUNTAINS

Celebrating the 100th Anniversary of R.L. Stevenson's birth

You from piers on West Street, the soot of New York,
flotsam and jetsam of the world's waste
throbbing in your lungs, the spittle of your days;
You to a cottage overlooking river ripples,
trout jumping in spring, mountains rising into clouds...
a brigantine over Baker and Scarface;
you briskly hiking to the village general store
for a few provisions, stoking the stove with logs,
ink in your well mushy with mountain winter,
violets and crocus slowly coming to your cheek.
Books aside, and fame, you reached out to Scotland
in the Adirondacks and smiled away the winter.

Well, I, too, entered from New York, Brooklyn to be
exact, and the piers there on Columbia—though
my strawberry vines have long been in these mountains,
roots going further back than any explorer
from a distant land. I, too, first looked from a tamarack
on Baker and Scarface from a cedar. The flotsam
in my lungs as well, disenchantment rather than tb,
an ebbing of sensation for fame a city can bestow.

You lived facing the doors of death, and I looked
into the freshness of young students pondering careers...
"Black rap" beating against my ears, basketballs
and hockey pucks striking into my year until
forgetfulness eases aging thoughts into crocus bloom
and Meg's daffodils that sit upon my desk.
I haven't climbed Baker yet or fished Saranac
but I promise you I shall—one morning,
once my tamarack and cedar spread shadows

over the heat of noon. I shall climb into mist
and air and be content to sit upon the steps
of your cottage and realize you, too, saw
the Saranac flow under ice and, later, leafed willow.

SKY WOMAN

In the night
I see her fall
sometimes
clutching vines
of ripe strawberries,
sometimes sweetgrass,
other times
seeds
which will sprout.
Always
loon or crane
fly with her.

1.
I imagine her standing
by the cauldron stirring,
her naked flesh spattered
by bubbling corn mush.
Dogs came from the dark,
wolves, to lick her flesh.
Blood runs from wounds
the dogs have made
with their sharp tongues.

She will mother me
for generations.
Her endurance ensures mine.

2.
He pulled a great tree by its roots
from the sky earth
and left a gaping hole showing
the dark. Waters rumbled.

She was enticed to look deep
into the hole. She clutched
her abdomen, the child she carried,
and fell...
Water birds attended her...loon,
crane, mallard. Turtle stretched,
quaked, rose to surface dark waters
and await her passage.

3.
She filled woods with trillium, baneberry;
she gave hawk flight, thrush song,
and seeded cedar and sumac.
She flecked her hand in cold waters
and fish came to nibble fingertips.
All about her was wonder.
She brought grains to the fields
and deer to sweet meadows;
she touched maples
and juices ran down the trunks;
she looked back/up and rains
fell...she brought surprise.

All this her grandsons made,
and the face in the mountain rock,
river currents, deadly nightshade,
forests of elm, tamarack, birch, white pine;
the little spirits and the red people;
wolf and wolverine and bear.
She brought delight...
the greenness of things.

This her grandsons knew,
the birthed twins—Sapling and Flint:
she brought beauty under nourishing sun

and illumination of the moon
and stars over winds blowing
from all directions.

I'll look
tonight
for her to fall
again
from among stars
with strawberries
or sweetgrass
held tightly in her hands.

STILL LIFE AT CEDAR HOUSE: CLOVER

For Meg, the painter–who cares

I eased
by it
in the summer morning;
autumn I lowered
the shade;
winter blows
across these Adirondacks:
it
remains in the drifts of snow.

Still tall—
though no longer steady—
browned
it trembles in the dawn.
December
light makes shadows,
catches
the dry bloom
paling magenta.

Night
comes down hard.
Shivers. Until spring—
forgotten.
By all the many eyes.

TONGUE-TIED

Stones are heavy.
As a matter of fact.
Like words which roll boulders
out of rusty memory;
mouth dulled and warped
by both politicians and instant oatmeal.
Cola corrodes the tongue.

Ice melts if held tightly.
Should you care to hold it.
Cold water will seep between fingers
as the scream bloods the air,
as the old stag, the buck, the hind
falls to winter and the gun shot.

His killer smiles
and tramps from the woods
for a cold beer or three.
Obviously the air was not bitter.

Stones are heavy...
depending upon the size.
Words which roll like boulders
down the steep slope of the chin
quivering in the cold.
The wind-factor was bitter.

Bury frost-bitten fingers
in the steaming blood
of the stiffening deer.

CUDWEED
Sometimes known as Owl's Crown

> "Rare Plants Found In Adirondacks"
> —Headline in the *Plattsburgh Press-Republican*

For Matt Kasson—who cares

sounds
like something
a white-tail chewed
in a back meadow
and spat out
naturalists
say you are rare
to these ol' mountains
Dr. Kudish calls you
       Gnaphalium Uliginosum
       is that Latin for ugly
never
       or almost never seen
       so maybe they are right
do you grow
       in hollows
       bogs
       the edge of ponds
       under tamaracks
       beside bunch berries
       or just on the lawn
       of the Paul Smith's campus
are you
       cousin to
       black-eyed-susans
       iris, hare-bells, fleabane
why

aren't you listed
in wildflower
guidebooks
are you
medicinal
edible, decorative
poison
has
Madeleine or Karen
pressed your petals
into frames
for safekeeping
do you bloom
nights with moonflowers
days as chicory
are you
red, white, blue
or yellow, pink, organdy
do
brides wear you
color coffins or graves
does wind
blow through your
September leaves and blooms
stars
twinkle on your petals
rain
drip through to roots
or
are you the unexplained mystery
of the Adirondack wolf;
cure-cottage ghost—
the young boy who visits kitchens
at night when the town
and all the cats sleep;

or the lost hiker
on the snowed slopes of Iroquois Peak
or Algonquin or in Indian Pass
are you really
common
as goldenrod, skunks, blackouts
who
are you
and where
can you
be seen
scented
survive
harsh winters
late springs
tourists' pluckings
scientists' prods
or poets' imaginations
ah!
you've escaped but perhaps
in danger
the foot must look-out for you
yet will it know
when it comes upon your stalk
as it wades through brush or bog
stands of witchhobble
significant meadows
of daisies and vetch
yes
hide
creep under vines
grow
tall so no hand can reach
& break your stem
drag

you screaming
into a crystal vase
or simply stomp
you dead

"It's not a very spectacular plant, but it's interesting
nevertheless and a welcome addition to our alpine flora."
—Dr. Richard Mitchel

indigenous, native
        weedy species
remind them
        there is no such thing
        as an ugly
        child or cat
survive
        on your alpine slope
        or on that campus
and
        persist
        like hawkweed, the beaver, moose
        and the Indian

CHOKEBERRY

When puckery kids we used to call
them chokecherries
as they spread through clearings,
blossoms April-pink, blossoms
which could tickle a boy's chin.
Black now in August as midnight,
they cluster, dangle afternoon,
bitter to tongue as wasp gall.
We wait for Kathleen to climb
the birch hill to gather
the fruit and with many cups
of sugar preserve summer
which bear and songbirds
devour once autumn's tinted
maple, beech and tamarack,
flames spotted here and there
on October's Adirondack hills.

Elderberry bellied to robins and swallows;
raspberries gone to seed and pies;
bear have stripped low branches
of blueberries, and now
only chokecherries offer a tease.

Kathleen, bring your berry can,
beat the robins to harvest
these fine last moments of summer,
fragile and sun-warm still...
as jewel-weed turns and falls
and mustard yellows
reflected against skies
rhythmed to mallard and loon
heading to hibiscus and orange blossoms.

INDOMITABLE SPIRIT

struggling into leaf
scraggling into bud
rain could not break your stalk
dry spells were not sufficient
to burn your essence
bees neglected you
care ignored your early mornings
winds beat you time and again
but today
this bright August morning
after a wicked thunder storm
you stand radiant to O'Keeffe's
ghostly brush
and Van Gogh's agony
the lemon of your petals
thrust out to answer...
the sunflower
with the stamina,
strength of a warrior;
indigenous
seeds once used for flour
by my ancient sisters,
oil which not only cooked
venison but wild turkey,
and handsomely dressed
the chief's hair
they turned you into washday soap
claimed, later, you
protected the people
from malaria—as legend goes

tallest flower of the fields
you guard the corn,

feed the ruby-throated
hummingbird
hornets and spiders
which crawl your stalk,
petals and seeds

spirit of wonder
and surprise
bulwark against the elements
you proudly color
the memory of summer
the pleasure of hands
working in the earth

for Bob Cook, farmer

STONE THROWING

He called out
hey you with the blue eyes
you can't be no Indian.

Well, that's what my
father said, too,
to my mother...
where did he get those blue eyes?

She just smiled.
and her smile said
none of your business,
and gave birth
to another child
As if to say
it is not the pale of blood
but what
the heart is made of.

Hey he called out
you don't have no
feather in your hair
That's right
I said when I grew
older,
and no rings
on my toes,
either.

What's your Indian
name he asked,
and hey speak some
of that language.

It's not a name
or words
that makes a man a man.
My reply finally
calmed his nerves
and I lit my pipe
quietly in the dark.
He left me alone then,
probably a little
confused,
but that's life.
I assured him
I could dance
but I wouldn't.

REFLECTED EBERHART

"Enigma rules, and the heart has no certainty."
                                                    —R.E.

I scent the old man's moccasins
corn of the field
trout of
the cold stream
deer and elderberry
of the woods
blood of war and ballet
smoke of peace
birth of colt
Penobscot, Mohawk
Lakota, Zuni, Pima
or Spokane

The moccasins dance
in the Longhouse, the Kiva, Hogan
in the leather they carry
feet hefting the weight
of civilization
once on the old man's shoulders
Cree, Anisnawbe
Cheyenne, Kiowa
Papago or Miwok

I scent the old man's moccasins
and smell the scent of man;
the flux continues to rise
snow of the sky
the rush of the river
June's strawberry blossom
        the fire of the village

GOLD

a lock, leaf, a ring
watch, meaningless date
penciled in black
on the wall calendar

yowl echoes
down dark halls
replaces
the cry
of stiff knees
and bent shoulders
though not broken

spirit reduced to a shuffle
as eyes search
the corner by the front door
for the cane, or
the young lad's sturdy arm

touching the bright hair
of memory's record
some lost face now
wrinkled
some lovely body
delicious to the touch, kiss
the golden light
of intellect
must sustain
surely Eberhart would agree

applause brings color
to the cheek
touch of bush cranberry

sky doubles with rainbows
as the last timber wolf
yowls

anticipation
surrendered
to the embrace
of yellow roses

framed into euphoria
recognition should
make for content
sniff the friendship
of the roses

the aster petals
pressed
within the covers
of the book
purple staining
facing pages

The meadow sits in the palm
with the hickory nut tree
and the sky has colored eyes
rainbow trout smile
from lips

faint night light
in the public house
of malcontent
or among children
public yet not public
think in parables
and dream of cold eyes

allow the dancer the dance
under heavy boughs
of black willow
bending below
double moon flooding
the road that only
the most precious can find

damaged
damaged daylight
damaged nightlight
unconnected bones
standing, standing in the museum
closed to the public
and school children
even though they might
hold tickets in hand
and the smell of lilac
mingled with the smell of rats
bloodied on broken glass

be contented the tooth
will not ache
feet not flatten
flesh not dry and wrinkle
and all desire, lust
is abated

there are those who say
the Indian is dead
vanished, vanquished
but listen to the radio
hear the drum
shake of the rattle
hear the keen of voices

eat pumpkin soup
drink strawberry juice
and be rejuvenated

gold
what is golden
amid the golden fields
no bones of death
what is golden
only the propaganda
the listless remembrance
of a June afternoon
which cannot return
after new rain
or a lament to St. Theresa

turn on the radio
the groundhog saw his shadow
so the children will go to school
turn on TV
bend and kiss the naked thigh
hear the whisper and sweaty groans
reflected in the photographic dream
allow the anger
to master the hand
moving toward the groin

lift up the glass
and be satisfied
the moon moves
across the sky

YOU KNOW WHO YOU ARE, WERE, WILL BE

I loved
the sound of your fingers
on the keys
spinning the web,
the scrape of the chair
pulled up to the machine.

I realized one day
you must close the door
on your smile/laugh.
Don't slam it too loudly
or you will shatter the web.

I will miss
the arguments
dark after darkness
falling on silver...
coffee after coffee
after juice after...

Though it won't happen
I will look forward
to the knuckle-knock
on the book/poem/anecdote/
mounds of tansy and smoke.

You must travel
a little
as I tear the webs
from velvet lids.

But don't walk
too far from the apple tree

where our names hang
in the spun gold,
with the names of
Keats/Rimbaud/Sappho.

You could be a thousand
upper-class students/
poets/lovers/editors/
garbage collectors
who nail trinkets to walls
and serve refuge at dinner
and collect spun lines.

You are the thousand
plain/pretty/handsome/ugly
faces who have sat
before me
spinning
before open texts
of bouillon/tomato paste/
gooseberry jam/pesto/clay
pitons/sleeping bags and such.

I'll remember
the shine of the words/magic
dangling on moonlight
always—so go but not far
in case I need you at noon
when limbs tire and eyes
grow dim on moon and rain
and morning glories wilt.

But did I tell you
the peppers hang on the plants
and how tasty they were

in the bean burrito?

—and that I had a postcard
from Seattle/Santa Fe/Baja/
San Francisco/ Bolivia/Cornell
and is doing just fine in all
places.

Go and be free
as blood rushing
your fingers pounding
the keys by which
you shall always
be.

The spider has found me.
Grandmother sucks the juice,
and the coffee, black and pungent,
streams from the eyes.
I will wake in your memory
and I shall carry you
into the sun forever.

Remember
to return
my books
someday.

Words To The Indian Woman Of The West Coast

Check, if you must,
the geography
of my palms—
lines of rivers
flowing out of the long
histories of my bloods,
pausing to quench
thirst of a tamarack

Check, if you will,
the crows
cawing in my eyes,
hawks singing in the heart
grass growing up the arms
the bent of the back
burdened with bags of tongues,
words cut from stones
rhythms too heavy
for darkness

My corn boils in blood
makes good bread
for long journeys;
my beans climb
to morning
where sun feeds roots
after April;
my squash ovens
in the empty belly
allows feet to dance
on summer
or the wood flooring
of a longhouse

when snow embraces
red willow and sumac

Pain by pain
we match—
your geography
does not differ
that much though sea
runs in your veins
and in mine mountain
spring waters

Raven darkens your night under cedar
cedar sings and heals in my country
and eagle soars high over pine and maple

Legends slip from your tongue
but we, too, carry stories
from the stone in our hands
to winter and the dawn of green corn
when strawberries scent evening air
and children are struck with awe and wonder

Check and balance—
if you must...

OKANAGAN

I, too, know this
geography
drawn in red lines
of both blood but
language first

I, too, know these
mountains
which rush with spring
runs of sweet water
and sweet blood

I, too, know this
orchard
of peaches...honey
to the tongue, yet
hung brave men

I, too, know this
salmon
from my polluted
veins now that child-
hood remembers
the baking

I know the winter
river
the summer canyon
the last howl
of wolf
spring growl
of bear

I know this earth
in moist hands

I know blood
which continues
to spill from
lips and palms

I know this fish
now turned to stone
which breaks teeth
and kills in the belly
still angry
with hunger...
frozen forever
now, maybe.

This typography
has been trekked
on hands and knees

pained and
bloodied

EL PASO DEL NORTE
March 8, 1984

> While observing two soldiers kiss goodbye in the
> Alamagordo, New Mexico, bus station.

Fourteen years later searching your blond smile
after writing poems, writing plays, waiting dreams,
a persistent love in the fleabag El Paso hotel;
sun-drenched streets of Juarez where you insisted
upon buying a white cowboy hat but made me happier
with your gift of a bull fight poster and a carton
of Delmonicos; dreaming you again
in these Juarez streets where you cautiously
refused sweet drinks of coconut, chocolate or rice
or the little rolled tacos as they shouted, "gringos,"
and offered prostitutes, or boys, to our laughter.

Those mountains rose, desert stretched, hot nights
crawled over sweat and the snot and weird graffiti
on the hotel room walls; our lives lit by a single bulb
dangling over the bed exposing your mole
and the map wandering your cheek and neck, sun-burnt,
my poems and stories littering the trail to Tuscon. I gave
your broken hands the stub of my one-way ticket
to San Francisco, and called you Pat Garrett: you shot
in the night under Arizona stars in the glow
of our cigarettes. I'm still waiting at the 7th Street
Station in the tenderloin for your arrival.

One day that bus will pull in with blond
smiles, while in the meantime I am in ol' El Paso
del Norte rummaging ghosts and whispers, writing dreams,
forgetting I'm bald and grey, forgetting you, too,
would be whiskered and not the stud/cowboy

from Utah on the southwest road selling opals
to tourists. I wonder if we could meet again
in the vagaries of aging. Would I pay half
the hotel rent, dropping my dollars on top of yours?
Age does slow the blood as mountain altitude slows gait,
allows fewer dreams and blunts vision.

My blood would not bubble sighting thighs,
wildflowers on your forehead, verbena in your hands.
I wouldn't shiver as my arm brushed your shoulder
passing to the john, nor eye catch my reflected
glance in the dirty mirror. We would both be afraid
or listless; we'd make no reckless move, eye contact
nor swell in the groin. Terror/age does this—
erases the stare that looks for cops instead
of secret places for love. You get comfortable
growing older, play safe moves, finger dirty books,
pictures, fantasize not dream, not imagine the
eruption of beauty, thrills, turnstile/turn
about for adventure to break prisms
into jewels: rubies and emeralds, yes, opals, or
star-bursts and iris, a night into a mere second, orgy
to agony. As a Jewish friend once said, "You know
you're old when a good shit feels better than sex."

I prefer to think you are still selling opals
or were knifed in some barroom/poolhall brawl.
Or maybe run an ice cream parlor in Carmel.
Perhaps you have fathered a dynasty, maybe
you have melted into dreams, an anecdote in the shape
of a poem. Maybe that's all you were—a poem.

In El Paso my blood rushes, slowed legs move
a little faster through the plaza giving an ear
to Spanish lips, giving an eye to Chicano thighs

as I search streets for your blond smiles,
the fleabag hotel whose name I can't remember.

I look off to the mountain peaks on the way
north to Albuquerque and think of Billy the Kid.
I probably won't pass thru El Paso again.

ALLEN GINSBERG
APRIL 5, 1997, 11 A.M.

I'm sitting here eating leftover
chicken pot pie...two days old.
Just stepped into the kitchen...where the radio
is running its mouth...from checking out
last year's day lily stalks—sand dry.
The yard is dotted with fresh holes—mouse
holes or mole tunnels—Lucy, our cat,
will discover with her sharp tartarless teeth.
Eating an early lunch because I rose early
to talk to Jamie just home from Baja
and he walks with heavy tales and tins of shells
and stones, I also rose early because the sun
promised to come out on the mountains, shine and melt
ice and snow with its fire which I personally
think it is time for winter to cut out. Cool!

I am avoiding the issue, reason why I hold this pen
and scratch over this legal tablet of yellow paper.
I will write it in a whisper—Allen Ginsberg died
of liver cancer this morning. No no no I won't
whisper. I will shout—
ALLEN GINSBERG DIED THIS MORNING AT 11 A.M.
This morning. This A.M.
An age died this morning of liver cancer.
Seventy years just passed into the earth.
I should go read "Kaddish," Naomi, even if I'm not
Jewish. "Kaddish"—one of Allen's great poems.
Oh my! What year was it that Fred and I—
Fred passed away of cancer last year—went to Brooklyn
Academy to see the production of Allen's "Kaddish"?
A night to remember.
                    Shit, Edna was right—life is

not much more than a progression of dead loved ones
passing down, down, down into the darkness, earth
before our eyes and hands and we can't stop this
parade.

How do I summon Edna's passion, compassion,
her anger, sense of loss, tragedy while I sit here
eating this soggy left-over chicken pot pie.
The incredulity. The irony. Why am I not
enraged.

I think he is probably right this moment
yakking with Blake and Jack and asking
for a cute boy angel of heaven and demanding the boss
up there legalize pot. Solomon and Rexroth
are lining out heaven's rules which Allen will break
almost immediately—Like: "Sweet boy, gimme
your ass."

Numbers of poets welcome him; Carl
Sagan said here are the stars, Allen. Spicer
was waiting and Neal smiled from ear to ear.
Is this why I can't/don't cry. I've
always said I cry at melodrama, never
at true tragedy. Yet, somewhere inside
demands rage I couldn't weep when Audre
died a few years ago either—surely out of
the shock, the total disbelief even though
we knew she was dying a fearful death, the disbelief
that this beautiful black, lesbian, feminist poet
woman died and now this beautiful Jewish, gay
male poet has pulled the Lower East Side shroud
up over his chin to cover his startled eyes.
I refuse to accept their deaths. Auden was right.
"The day of his death was a dark cold day."
All the waters were frozen and the airports
should have been closed and all the altars
adorned with the red roses which Edna said

they had gone to feed.
                    A chill has touched
the sunlight and a snappy wind whips the scarf
about my throat/edges of my shoulders.

Allen wouldn't want a pail of tears.
He'd most likely say, read a poem, say a prayer
and go fuck a fat boy.
                    Nonetheless
the clouds are lowered; the year has come to an end,
poems bouquet Louie's waiting hand.

ANDREW'S DILEMMA

Thinking of Andrew
stuck in the snow
on an old farm road
with a bottle of water
and a plastic container
of leftover
Chinese noodles and sauce.

A year later, last
night, he said
he wished
they had not pulled
his truck out of the snow,
and that he was forever stuck
because his brother
would still eat
tacos and would
continue to
film Ninja Turtles
and not be rotting
in a grave from cancer.

Set back
time,
he said.

FEO/BELLO

Ugly is covered with beauty—
colors of winter—purples
and blues, ochre wash, and
January white not yet stained
by afternoon, nor hidden by night
and the lies perpetrated
against innocence.

One blue spruce bends
under a heavy load of snow;
one red cardinal's brilliant
wings float over morning
and bring excitement to day;
thrill of children making
snowmen with prune eyes and
broccoli noses.

Creek frozen for sharp skates
to whish down snowed meadows
to church or store or neighbor's
chocolate cake and cocoa date;
creek winding a winter song
across the landscape, lyrics
few will hear, or want to hear.

Cruel in many ways: winter
bites toes, fingers and noses
but worse it takes the breath of
an aged man struggling home
with a bag of meal on his back
for the dog too old to rabbit hunt;
cruel to the bluejay lost in a storm
from nest; cruel to the young

girl with blue ribbons in her hair
floundering in the storm, her way
home from toting surprise to grandma;
to the ancient house leaning in
harsh winds which bring down
rafters and crack windowpanes...
a house that once was the home of
joy and parties and newborns
from young love; barns of
fertile horses and their foals.
Winter, new snow hides the ugly,
allows beauty before it is stained,
blizzard in the colors of night

EXISTENTIAL DREAD

What an Indian has to say about the work of Bacon
1/29/99

Francis,
only two months ago
the *New York Times*
reported on your
"nasty, delicious
beauty."
What say there,
ol' fellow,
wild artist,
most of the world—
when I was young and impressionable
and recognized only greatness
which suited my needs—
thought your canvas not
good enough to wrap
fish in let alone
purchase and hang
on a living room wall
where little kids might giggle
and gramps might up-chuck
the spaghetti supper.
But now you hang in good places;
ministers in black gowns
may speak openly of your
deliciousness
and advise the congregation
to buy tickets for the show.
Don't forget the "Screaming Pope."

And don't forget he posed, Bacon's
lover naked on a stool

centered in an empty studio
below a dangling lightbulb
as if in a fleabag hotel
not too different from
some folks' shitty lives.

"Sensuous paint"—
that if touched would stick
to the fingertip;
the scent of the paint
never to leave your nostrils,
recollection.
The touch will torment
as surely you would have touched
the torment in paint
Francis caught
in light and shadow
in red and black—
red of blood,
black of hell.
These lone figures, "isolated"
in the center of activity
the middle of day
colored in rainbows
but scented by a splash
of sour lemon.
George Dyer, the lover,
committed the brave
act of suicide
obviously
in nasty, delicious beauty—
"ultimately dazzling."

Lush language
for lush paintings.

I almost wrote *pain*
which comes so easy
when thinking, reconsidering
the genius. And
it does dazzle, it
is delicious
but bitter,
agonizing.

As Kahlo was reported
to have said—
"I'm not a Surrealist,
I never painted dreams.
I painted my own
reality."
Surely this sentiment
could have been uttered
by Francis
sometime before
he died in '92

We forget Michelangelo's sweat
and Vincent's deaf ear
which first he cut
and then shot himself
by the blast of his gun.
We forget Cezanne's
frustration.
the loneliness he must
have suffered
for just a tad more
than comradeship.

Now that Britain
has acclaimed

it can forget how it
vilified
the early labors
as "horror, disconcerting."

Wait until death,
and what now they may think
of as toilet paper
will be valued
in millions and thought
of as
"delicious."

Detail

Francis Bacon's "Study of George Dyer"

Forget he's sitting on a stool,
nude;
pay no attention to his
countenance;
disregard his feet resting on
newspaper.
Nasty.
George took his life that year.
But look beyond;
be a proper critic
and seize
the day—
observe
the naked leg
raised but bent
in the doorway
of the room beyond
where George sits
painted in magenta
his face distorted
in love yet discontent.
Is that Francis, himself
waiting for George
to come to bed.
The strong muscle
of these limbs—
tough, sinewy
though aging
into welfare
of the spirit—
no abstraction for him,
either

as death and love and bed
are real not the surrealism
existentialism
critics find.
The crucifix melts
in dripping blood
as the painting hangs
on the wall
as the painter rots
evolving into
a newborn pup
which will grow up
and piss on the world.

MAURICE KENNY: A BRIEF BIOGRAPHY

Born in Watertown in New York State's North Country on August 16, 1929, to Andrew Anthony and Doris Marie Parker Herrick Kenny, Maurice Kenny grew up in the foothills of the Adirondack Mountains with his parents and two older sisters, Agnes and Mary. When he was thirteen years old, his parents separated and he moved to Bayonne, New Jersey, with his mother and his sister Mary. Despising school there, where he was made to feel like an outcast, Kenny often spent his lunch money on a bus trip across the Hudson River to Manhattan, a place he came to love.

The number of school days skipped brought Kenny before a judge who recommended a reform school for truant boys. Upon learning this, Kenny's father arrived and took him back to the North Country to live. During his high school years, he returned to New York City as often as finances allowed. After graduating from high school, Kenny, who was always filled with wanderlust, hitchhiked to North Carolina to visit the Thomas Wolfe homesite in Asheville. From there, he hitchhiked on to New Orleans, intending to go to Mexico. Having very little money, he instead wandered along the Mississippi River to St. Louis, where his eldest sister, Agnes, and her husband lived. He spent several months with them before heading east to Indianapolis, where, in 1952, he enrolled at Butler University as a "special student."

He was, Kenny states, "soon indoctrinated by the Keats scholar Werner Beyer and the religious poet Roy Marz," who told Kenny he should give up poetry and try fiction. Kenny immediately set to work on a novel. Unhappy with it upon its completion, he left Butler and, with the aid of his father, traveled back to his North Country home. There, in 1956, he entered St. Lawrence University and took a course from novelist Douglas Angus. "He almost instantly persuaded me back to poetry, and I will always be thankful to him." The result was the chapbook *The Hopeless Kill*. His father urged him to return to New York City and attend Columbia University, and Kenny applied, took the entrance exam and passed. Upon arrival in New York, however, he needed to find a means of support and took a job at the Marboro Book Shop. Several months later, he was promoted to manager and decided to postpone resuming his education.

In 1958, his father died, and Kenny decided to enter New York University to study with poet Louise Bogan. He lived in a loft on Bleecker Street and worked at a series of jobs to pay the rent. "There was a sparkle in the air at that time, and a few of those sparks ignited me," Kenny has said. With Bogan's guidance, Kenny published work in several journals and magazines and, in 1958, his first full-length collection of work, *Dead Letters Sent*, as well as the chapbooks *With Love to Lesbia* (1958) and *And Grieve, Lesbia* (1960).

After leaving New York University, Kenny again felt the need to wander and he traveled extensively to California, the Southwest, Mexico, and on to Puerto Rico and the Virgin Islands, where he settled on St. Thomas and began to drink heavily. He wrote very little during these years, although he did see one poem published in the *New York Times*. Eventually, friends from New York flew to St. Thomas to rescue him from his beach bar existence and returned him to New York. Following a brief stay, he set off for Chicago. He stepped off the airplane on a cold December morning and then spent one year there, where he wrote obituaries for the *Sun-Times* to earn a living while writing numerous poems. He returned to New York City in 1967, found a rent-controlled apartment in Brooklyn Heights and a job as a waiter at a posh Park Avenue discothèque. He remained in that job until a heart attack forced him to leave in 1974.

Akwesasne Notes, a journal of the Akwesasne Reserve in Northern New York State, printed a long poem Kenny had penned in 1973 as a response to the confrontation between members of the American Indian Movement and federal agents at Wounded Knee, North Dakota. Based on a chant from the Ghost Dance religion, a movement among many tribes in the late 1800s that attempted to resurrect the past spiritually and physically through songs and dances, the poem marked the beginning of Kenny's determination to bring Native American culture into the literary canon. To further this effort, he established Strawberry Press in 1976 to publish Native American writers. He also worked during the '70s as editor of the influential journal *Contact II*, which published many writers outside academe, including many minority writers.

I Am the Sun was published as a pamphlet by Dodeca in 1976. In 1977, Kenny's first full-length collection in nineteen years, *North: Poems of Home*, appeared. More books followed, all with strong Native themes: *Dancing Back Strong the Nation*, 1979; *Only as Far as Brooklyn*, 1981; *Kneading the Blood*, 1981; *Boston Tea Party*, 1981; and *The Smell of Slaughter*, 1982. In 1982, Kenny also published *Blackrobe: Isaac Jogues*, his first venture into historical poetry. This story in voices, which was nominated for a Pulitzer Prize, tells of the Jesuit priest Isaac Jogues and his relationship with the Mohawk people he was trying to convert. The book made it clear that American history is also Native history and demonstrated the importance of listening to more than one voice. *Blackrobe* also received the National Public Radio for Broadcasting Award.

Following the death of his mother, Kenny began to work through his grief in a series of poems that became the exquisite, extended elegy, *The Mama Poems*, which won the coveted American Book Award given by the Before Columbus Foundation in 1984. Kenny followed that with *Is Summer This Bear*, a paean to the Adirondack North Country where Kenny was now spending part of the year. Also in 1985, Kenny turned his voice once again to fiction and published *Rain and Other Fiction*, a collection of short stories and a one-act play.

Throughout these years, Kenny had been traveling, giving poetry readings and spending extended lengths of time away from New York teaching at various colleges and universities. In 1986 he decided to give up his beloved apartment in Brooklyn Heights and live full time in Saranac Lake in the Adirondacks, where he was teaching at North Country Community College. In 1987, White Pine Press published *Between Two Rivers: Selected Poems, 1956-1984*. *Humors and/or Not So Humorous* also appeared in 1987, *Greyhounding this America* in 1988, *The Short and Long of It* in 1990, and *Last Mornings in Brooklyn* in 1991.

In 1992, White Pine Press published *Tekonwatonti: Molly Brant*. Similar to *Blackrobe* in that it is an historical work in voices, the book traces the life of Tekonwatonti, sister of famed Mohawk Joseph Brant and wife of the legendary Sir William Johnson. Molly was destined to be little more than a footnote to history; Kenny felt he had to tell her story and assure her rightful place as a heroine in American history. The book took twelve years to write, and there is little doubt that Kenny considers it his most important work.

Throughout the 1990s, Kenny continued to travel and teach at various places, including St. Lawrence University and Paul Smith's College in upstate New York, the University of Victoria in British Columbia, Lehigh University, and the University of Oklahoma. In 1995, St. Lawrence University honored Maurice Kenny with the degree of Doctor of Literature. Kenny published *On Second Thought: A Compilation*, in 1995 and a collection of essays, *Backward to Forward*, in 1997. *Common Days: A Place Record* appeared in 1998 and *In the Time of the Present* in 2000. His work frequently appears in magazines, journals and anthologies. He is also editor of *Wounds Beneath the Flesh: Native American Poetry* (1983) and *Stories for a Winter's Night: Short Fiction by Native American Writers* (2000). Kenny presently lives in Saranac Lake, New York, and teaches at the State University of New York College at Potsdam.